ICE CREAM

Irresistible frozen desserts to make at home

igloobooks

Published in 2017
by Igloo Books Ltd
Cottage Farm
Sywell
NN6 0BJ
www.igloobooks.com

Original book title: Gelato Chez Moi

Socio Unico Giangiacomo Feltrinelli Editore srl
Via Andegari 6 - 20121 Milano
info@gribaudo.it
www.feltrinellieditore.it/gribaudo/

The measurements used are approximate.

Text and photographs by Barbara Torresan

LEO002 0517
2 4 6 8 10 9 7 5 3 1
ISBN 978-1-78557-272-2

Cover designed by Nicholas Gage
Interiors designed by Charlie Wood-Penn
Edited by Bobby Newlyn-Jones

Printed and manufactured in China

Ingredients

Dairy

The classic ice creams are milk and/or cream based. Both should preferably be fresh and whole, with 3.5 per cent fat for milk and a minimum of 35 per cent fat for cream. There is no reason not to use raw whole milk, as long as you do not have anything against it yourself. It is important to know that skimmed milk and cream with a lower fat content could change the consistency of the ice cream itself, forcing us to use thickeners that it would be better to avoid. In many recipes in this book, you will find condensed milk, which, owing to its natural creaminess and sweetness, is a perfect base, especially for ice cream prepared without using an ice cream maker. If you prefer to avoid cow's milk, you can also use goat's milk, remembering that it has a much stronger flavour. Therefore, all the other ingredients in the recipe will have to be adjusted to taste. Another alternative is plant milk.

Sweeteners

There are a wide variety of sweeteners, from simple caster sugar to the various cane and unrefined sugars, sugar syrups, glucose and honey. The recipes show the weight of sugar and you can then decide to opt for the possible variations based on your personal taste, including alternative sugars and natural sweeteners. Obviously, in this case, go ahead and taste it until you find the ideal flavour.

Juicing

Juicing requires a certain level of commitment, but the long-term payoff for your health is well worth it. Firstly, you will need to invest in a juicer. Next, in order to get the most out of your juicer, it is helpful to maintain a fresh supply of fruits and vegetables. Having an abundance and variety of produce on hand means you can fulfil any craving or health need in seconds. If you have a busy schedule, you may find juicing easier and even more enjoyable when you have a whole range of juices within arm's reach. Most juices will stay fresh for up to three days in the refrigerator, or for longer in the freezer, so you can plan ahead if you have a busy schedule. If you do choose to freeze your juices, remember they will need a few hours in the refrigerator to thaw. Finally, start experimenting! By mixing and matching ingredients, you will soon learn what tastes good and the variations of juices you enjoy.

Fresh fruit, nuts and herbs and spices

The best fruits are those that are in season and must be strictly healthy and ripened to the right degree. If possible, use raw fruit to maintain the flavour and colour. With nuts, it is better to shell them upon use. If that is not possible, check that they are organic and free of preservatives. The flavours used in homemade ice cream should not be artificial. In the following recipes, vanilla pods are used from which you will need to extract the fragrant seeds. The same goes for aromatic herbs. For these recipes, fresh herbs are used that are left to infuse. In this way, they will release all their aroma and you will not need to resort to bottles and sachets.

Vegan Ice Creams

If you do not like milk or are vegan, you can still have ice cream. There are excellent cow's milk and cream substitutes, including almond, soy, rice, oat and coconut milk and plant creams.

To make the ice cream creamy, like those made with traditional milk and cream, glucose syrup can be used instead of sugar and, if necessary, carob powder, agar-agar or guar flour. Vegan ice cream does not contain animal protein or fat.

The proteins in milk and cream capture the majority of the free water, therefore preventing it from forming large ice crystals. The fat in egg yokes and cream give the ice cream body and creaminess, as well as "warming" it to the palate. Both the fats and the proteins also stabilize the air that the mixture encapsulates during whipping. Both ensure that the ice cream succeeds in holding the air better, making the softness and lightness of the product last longer.

Therefore, because milk and cream are not used in vegan ice cream, it will naturally be less creamy, less aerated and will often have larger ice crystals. Below are some suggestions to try out and natural ingredients that could help you to obtain a result that is more similar to traditional ice cream. These ingredients are usually available in large food shops.

For creaminess, you can try using inulin. This is a vegetable fibre, mainly extracted from chicory. Although it will not be like fat, which gives ice cream that delicate velvety texture, inulin is a good alternative to use in vegan ice cream.

Inulin is a prebiotic fibre that has many benefits including lowering cholesterol, improving colonic transit and promoting the growth of beneficial intestinal bacteria. In sorbets that are low in fibre (such as lemon sorbet), it is very important.

Generally speaking, inulin can help to add creaminess and structure back into vegan ice cream and will replace the missing fats.

In sorbets, 2 per cent of the total weight is used. For example, if a mixture weighs 800 g, 2 per cent of this weight is added in inulin. Whereas, in vegan ice creams, this percentage can safely be increased to 3–4 per cent of the total weight. However, given that inulin is a substantial fibre, it is not advisable to go over 10 per cent, as you will risk the ice cream being excellent but also laxative!

Pectin can also be used. In sorbets, it is often already present in the fruit. The percentage to use ranges from 0.3 per cent to 0.5 per cent of the total weight of the mixture.

Many of the recipes in this book are vegan. These are easily identifiable as they will have a "vegan" label next to them.

Preparation: Granitas and Ice Lollies

Granitas and ice lollies are water-based. They are delicious, thirst-quenching and do not make us feel so guilty because they generally do not contain many calories.

Typically, all you need to do is add juice, syrup or an extract to ice to create a tasty dessert. From the simple ice lolly, made by adding juice to water, to the granita, which is made by using an ordinary mixer to break up the ice, which is then coloured with juices and syrups.

Alternatively, you can make granitas by preparing the desired flavour, freezing it in ice cube trays and, once it has frozen, crushing the ice cubes in an ice crusher.

Lastly, working strictly by hand and with a great deal of patience, we come to the "Sicilian" granita, which is often confused with sorbet owing to its creamy and very special structure. Hand whipping every 40 minutes will transform a base made up of just a few ingredients into an unparalleled delight.

To make the granita-making process easier, you can also use an ice cream maker, if it has a programme for granitas.

1. Place the ice in the ice crusher.

4. For "handmade" Sicilian granita, place the syrup in the freezer and beat it every 30 minutes.

2. Pour the crushed ice into a cup.

3. Add syrups or fruit juices.

5. Whipped granita.

6. To make ice lollies, use special moulds made of silicon.

Preparation: Fruit sorbets

Granita and gremolata are sometimes confused with sorbet, but sorbet is set apart from these owing to its consistency, which is more similar to that of ice cream.

Sorbet is a chilled, spoonable dessert that was invented perhaps even before ice cream. It is normally water and fruit based, although liqueurs are sometimes also used, lowering the freezing temperature and making the sorbet even softer.

In some restaurants, it is customary to serve sorbet between courses – generally between meat and fish courses – in particularly long meals, in order to aid digestion. Nowadays, it is also a very popular dessert, often chosen to replace a heavier, unhealthy dessert.

If you do not use a sorbet maker, it is important to remember to whip the sorbet once an hour with an electric whisk. By doing so, it will remain soft and fluffy.

Sometimes it is nice to change the way you serve sorbet to guests. One option is to whizz your sorbet in a blender for a few seconds, then dilute it with sparkling water. This mixture can then be served in champagne flutes or wine glasses.

1. Basic ingredients for lemon sorbet: water, lemon and sugar.

2. Prepare a syrup with water and sugar, then add the lemon juice.

3. Pour into the pre-cooled ice cream maker.

4. The sorbet should be ready in 20 minutes.

1. Ingredients for chocolate ice cream with white chocolate chips: chocolate, milk, cream, sugar.

2. The chocolate cream obtained by heating all the ingredients.

3. The ice cream takes on body in the ice cream maker.

4. Chocolate ice cream ready to eat.

Preparation: Ice cream with an Ice Cream Maker

There are many different kinds of ice cream maker: the simplest ones, the ones that take up least room and those that have a removable bowl that must be left in the freezer for at least 24 hours before use. Generally speaking, the bowl is then inserted into the base, where an electric paddle will whip the ice cream.

There are also automatic ice cream makers on the market. These are often more expensive, but they have an internal cooling system, therefore it is not necessary to cool the bowl in the freezer and they are generally equipped with a timer. These automatic ice cream makers are often very easy to use and great for when you have other meals to prepare at the same time – once you put the ingredients in, they will complete the whole ice cream making process by themselves.

Ice cream makers often include a tool or programme for making sorbets. However, given the variety of models, read the instructions of your ice cream maker and follow them carefully, using the ingredients suggested in the various recipes in this book.

Once the programme has finished, the ice cream is ready to eat. Any leftover ice cream can be kept in the freezer like any normal ice cream that you purchase.

Preparation: Non-frozen Ice Cream made with a planetary mixer

There are various models of planetary mixer, all with different settings and tools. As a basic element, all models are equipped with a whisk, which is the main accessory you will use to beat the ice cream. When using a planetary mixer, always make sure all of your ingredients are well-chilled and beat them for several minutes to ensure they are fully mixed.

In practice, the mixer replaces the handmade method. If you do not have a planetary mixer, you can always use an electric whisk. In the case of using an electric whisk, you should ensure you whisk the mixture well, but then also whisk it once every hour for three hours while it is cooling. This will help to maintain its creaminess.

1. The planetary mixer, ready with all the ingredients: instant coffee, condensed milk, cream and vanilla extract.

2. The finished mixture must be light and fluffy but firm.

3. Coffee ice cream, ready for freezing.

4. Soft and creamy after freezing.

Preparation: Custard Ice Cream (with egg)

This base can be used for custard, vanilla, zabaione, rum and raisin, tiramisu and all the other flavours that have a neutral creamy base.

350 ml / 14 fl. oz / 1 ½ cups milk
100 ml / 3 ½ fl. oz / ½ cup fresh cream
100 g /3 ½ oz / ½ cup sugar
75 g / 3 oz / 1/3 cup egg yolks
40 ml / 1 ¾ fl. oz / ¼ cup condensed milk

1. In a mixing bowl, combine the egg yolks and sugar.
2. Use the whisk to beat them until they are light and fluffy.
3. Add the cooled milk to the egg mixture in a slow steady trickle.
4. Heat to 85°C / 185F and simmer for 5 minutes, mixing and maintaining the temperature.
5. When the eggs have blended well with the sugar, add the milk, having first heated it to 80°C / 175F.
   Then, return the mixture to the heat and simmer at 85°C / 185F for around 4–5 minutes.
6. When the custard has cooled, add the lightly whipped cream and place the mixture in the freezer. Beat it manually at intervals or use an ice cream maker.

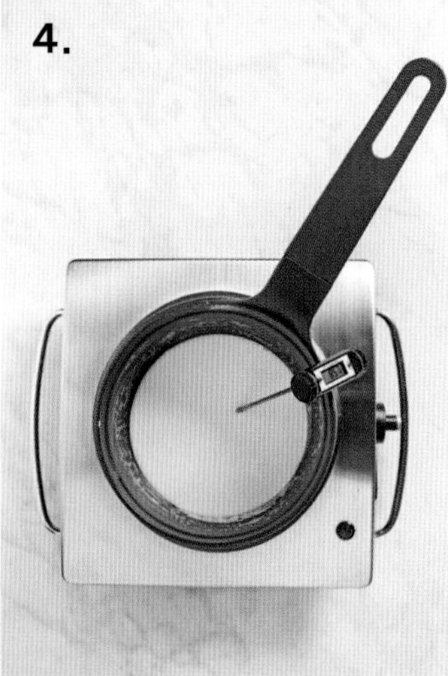

Preparation:
White Ice Cream

This base can be used for fiordilatte (whole dairy milk ice cream), stracciatella and for all dairy ice creams that do not contain egg, such as walnut, pistachio and coffee and also flavours like white chocolate and mascarpone.

300 ml / 10 fl. oz / 1 ¼ cups milk
300 ml / 10 fl. oz / 1 ¼ cups cream
100 g / 3 ½ oz / ½ cup sugar
40 ml condensed milk

1. Heat the sugar in a saucepan for just 1 minute.
2. Add the milk and heat it to 50–55°C/120–130F.
3. Add the cream and condensed milk, beating it with the whisk.
4. Cool and place it in the fridge before mixing with the ice cream maker.

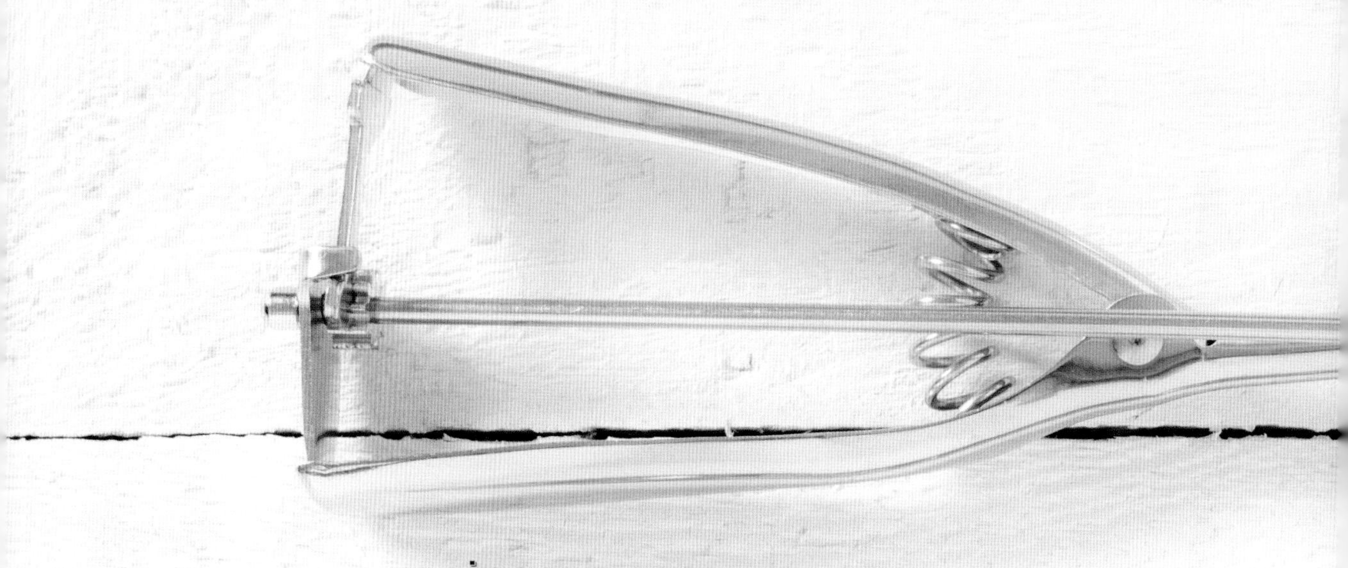

The **recipes** in this book are all written to serve 4, 6 or 8 people.
For the ice lollies, of course, it all depends on the size of your moulds. You can find little moulds that are very practical and convenient on the market, some of which are made of silicon.

As mentioned above, the ice cream must be **beaten thoroughly**,
particularly if you are not planning to use an ice cream maker.

It is also important to use **very cold ingredients**
and final containers in glass or steel that are deep enough to allow you to whip the ice cream in the intermediate freezing phases. Once it is ready, you can transfer the ice cream into small containers or special moulds if you want to create special shapes. Then finish the freezing phase.

Before the ice cream freezes completely, if you are not using moulds for ice creams on sticks, it is important to divide it **into portions** and keep it in several small containers, ideally with lids. Alternatively cover them with cling film or aluminium foil.

The difference between professional and homemade ice cream lies in the fact that additives and stablisers are used in many professional and shop-bought ice creams, hence homemade ice cream tends to **melt quicker** and is more affected by rapid changes in temperature.

The preparation and freezing times

These are indicated in the recipes in this book; refer to manual preparation. If you are using an ice cream maker, the times are considerably reduced. It is important to follow the instructions on your ice cream maker.

The **serving temperature** is also very important. Ideally, an hour or so before serving the ice cream, transfer it from the freezer to the fridge. If you forget, one controversial method is to place the ice cream in the microwave for 30 seconds at the highest power, so as to melt just its core to allow you to serve it more easily.

GRANITAS AND ICE LOLLIES

Fruits of The Forest Sicilian Granita

Preparation time + freezing for ideal consumption: 5-6 hours

Ingredients for 6-8

100 ml / 3 ½ fl. oz / ¼ cup orange juice

100 ml / 3 ½ fl. oz / ¼ cup lemon juice

150 g / 5 oz / ⅔ cup unrefined cane sugar

100 ml / 3 ½ fl. oz / ¼ cup water

600 g / 21 oz / 3 ¾ cups of mixed berries

Leave the berries to soak in the orange and lemon juices and half of the sugar.

In small saucepan, bring the water and remaining sugar to the boil. As soon as the sugar has dissolved, pour the mixture onto the mixed berries.

Using a stick blender, blend the mixture to create a purée.

Pour into a suitable container and place in the freezer, taking care to mix it every 40 minutes for at least the first 4 hours, so as to obtain a smooth and well-blended granita.

This granita is perfect for serving with whole berries and a brioche for a quick snack.

Grape and Prosecco Frozen Aperitif

Alcoholic ice lollies, only for grown-ups! You can prepare them the day before too.

Preparation time + freezing for ideal consumption: 12 hours

Ingredients for 4-6

220 ml / 7 ½ fl. oz / 1 cup white grape juice

80 ml / 2 ¾ fl. oz / ⅓ cup prosecco

200 ml / 6 ¾ fl. oz / ¾ cup water

fresh lemon juice

To obtain a good grape juice, use fresh grapes (at least 1 kg / 35 oz) and put the grapes through a juicer. Alternatively, you can find grape juice on the market with no added sugar and no preservatives.

In a jug, mix the prosecco, water and grape juice, add the lemon juice and pour into your chosen moulds.

Leave to freeze.

Serve after a meal as a light dessert. These frozen aperitifs are fresh and can aid digestion.

Peach and Raspberry Lollies

These ice lollies are very bright and cheerful. It is possible prepare them alternating the colours or you can make them multicoloured, freezing a few spoons of the blended fruit at a time.

Preparation time + freezing for ideal consumption: 8 hours

Ingredients for 4-6

1 lemon, juiced

250 ml / 9 fl. oz / 1 cup water

150 g / 5 oz / 1 ¼ cups yellow peach flesh

100 g / 3 ½ oz / ¾ cup raspberries

1 tbsp granulated sugar (optional)

Pour the lemon juice into the water and mix well.

Blend the peach with 150 ml / 5 fl. oz of the water and juice mixture. Pour the mixture into the moulds, filling them only half way. Place them in the freezer for about an hour, so that they cool rapidly.

In the meantime, blend the raspberries with the remaining water. Taste the raspberry mixture and if it is too sour, add a teaspoon of sugar if desired.

Pour the raspberries onto the peach base, which will already have hardened slightly and place the moulds back into the freezer for a few hours.

Kiwi Lollies

If you do not like celery juice, which adds a fresh and tangy element to these ice lollies, use water in the same quantities.

Preparation time + freezing for ideal consumption: 8 hours

Ingredients for 4-6

150 g / 5 oz / 1 ¼ cups kiwi flesh

100 ml / 3 ½ fl. oz / ½ cup lemon juice + grated zest

50 g /1 ¾ oz / ¼ cup sugar

100 ml / 3 ½ fl. oz / ½ cup water

100 ml / 3 ½ fl. oz / ½ cup green celery juice

Blend the kiwi with lemon juice.

Dissolve the sugar in the hot water and leave to boil for a couple of minutes.

Combine the syrup obtained, celery juice and fruit then blend again.

Pour the mixture into the moulds. If you like, add little slices of kiwi, cut finely to create a beautiful decorative effect.

Leave the ice lollies in the freezer for a few hours before eating them.

Melon Granita

This granita the perfect summer snack or a refreshing dessert after a meal.

Preparation time + freezing for ideal consumption: 5-6 hours

Ingredients for 4-6

100 ml / 3 ½ fl. oz / ½ cup water

100 g / 3 ½ oz / ½ cup sugar

handful mint leaves

350 g / 12 oz / 2 ¾ cups melon flesh

In a small pan, combine the water and sugar and mix, bring to the boil and leave to simmer for a minute. Turn off the heat, leave to cool for a moment and then add a few mint leaves.

Leave to rest until the syrup cools completely, then remove the mint and add the blended melon.

Mix and place in a glass or steel container and then place in the freezer.

For the first three hours, mix the granita every 40 minutes with a fork to blend it well.

Finally, beat with a spoon, leave it to harden and, with a special melon baller, extract lots of little balls and serve with a few sprigs of thyme. Alternatively, you can blend the granita roughly and serve it decorated with a few mint leaves.

Lemongrass Granita

This granita is excellent for aiding digestion, owing to both the lime and lemongrass and, above all, the ginger. Taste it during preparation and check whether the flavour is coming through sufficiently; if necessary, add another piece.

Preparation time + freezing for ideal consumption: 5-6 hours

Ingredients for 4-6

1 stick of lemon grass

300 ml / 10 fl. oz / 1 ¼ cups water

150 g / 5 ¼ oz / ⅔ cup sugar

200 ml / 6 ¾ fl. oz / 1 cup lime juice

1 cm fresh grated ginger

Cut the lemongrass from end to end, take off the first leaf and slice it or beat it with a rolling pin or the handle of a knife to release the scent.

In a small pan, mix water and sugar, bring to the boil, leave it to simmer for a minute, then turn off the heat, add the lemongrass, leave it to cool for a few minutes and add the lime juice and the finely grated ginger.

When the mixture has reached room temperature, sieve it, place it in a glass or steel container and place it in the freezer.

For the first 4 hours, mix the granita with a fork every 40 minutes to make it smooth. If you prefer a consistency similar to that of sorbet, pour the mixture into the ice cube trays and freeze.

Finally, place the ice cubes in an ice crusher at the highest power and mix carefully before serving.

Lemon and Lime Lollies

Preparation time + freezing for ideal consumption: 12 hours

Ingredients for 4-6

150 ml / 5 fl. oz / ¾ cup lime juice

150 ml / 5 fl. oz / ¾ cup lemon juice

grated zest of unwaxed lemon and lime

150 g / 5 oz / ⅔ cup sugar

200 ml / 6 ¾ fl. oz / 1 cup water

Wash the citrus fruits well and grate the rind, then squeeze them and sieve the juice.

Place the sugar in a pan, mix it with water, add the zest and bring to the boil. Leave it to simmer for a minute, then turn off the heat and leave it to cool.

Add the juice to the syrup, mix well and pour into the moulds.

Complete with a wooden stick and leave to cool.

Blood Orange Granita

Preparation time + freezing for ideal consumption: 5-6 hours

Ingredients for 4-6

100 g / 3 ½ oz / ½ cup sugar

150 ml / 5 fl. oz / ¾ cup water

zest of 2 unwaxed oranges

350 ml / 11 ¾ fl. oz / 1 ½ cups blood orange juice

240ml / 8 ¼ fl. oz / 1 cup orange liqueur

In a small pan, slowly melt the sugar in the water, then add the grated zest, bring to the boil and leave to reduce slightly. Turn off the heat and leave to cool.

In the meantime, add the orange juice to the cooled syrup, add the liqueur and mix well.

Divide into ice trays and leave to freeze. Lastly, in a mixer at the highest power or in an ice crusher, work the granita until the ice is crushed to the desired level.

Serve it accompanied with slices of orange.

Coffee Granita

This granita must be prepared by hand to achieve the ideal graininess and avoid the coffee separating from the sugar syrup.

Preparation time + freezing for ideal consumption: 5-6 hours

Ingredients for 4-6

250 ml / 8 ¾ fl. oz / 1 cup coffee (prepared with a mocha pot)

250 ml / 8 ¾ fl. oz / 1 cup water

100 g / 3 ½ oz / ½ cup sugar

1 vanilla pod

250 ml / 8 ¾ fl. oz / 1 cup fresh whipping cream (optional)

Prepare the coffee and leave it to cool.

In the meantime, place the water and sugar in a small pan together with the vanilla pod (cut along the length of the pod and open it like a book). Bring to the boil and leave to simmer for a minute until you have a syrup.

Sieve, add the coffee syrup and leave to cool completely, mixing from time to time.

When the mixture has reached room temperature, place it in a glass or steel container and place it in the freezer.

For the first 4 hours, mix the granita with a fork every 40 minutes to make it smooth.

Once it is ready, serve it with a generous spoonful of whipped cream.

When using just a few ingredients, it is best to choose excellent quality: good coffee and very fresh cream.

Cassis Lollies

Multiply the amounts if you want a lot of ice lollies, for an evening with friends, for example. Prepare them the day before serving. This is definitely an ice lolly for adults only, as Cassis contains alcohol. For children, blend the blueberries with water and sugar.

Preparation time + freezing for ideal consumption: 12 hours

Ingredients for 6-8

125g / 4 ⅓ oz / ¾ cup fresh blueberries

50 g / 1 ¾ oz / ¼ cup sugar

juice of 1 lemon

100 ml / 3 ½ fl. oz / ½ cup Cassis

250 ml / 9 fl. oz / 1 cup water

Rinse the blueberries under running water and leave them to rest covered with half of the sugar and the lemon juice.

Pour the Cassis, water and remaining sugar into a jug and mix to dissolve the sugar.

Distribute the blueberries with the liquid into the ice lolly moulds.

Cover the mixture with water and Cassis.

Cover with aluminium foil or the cover supplied and insert the wooden sticks.

Lastly, place in the freezer for at least 12 hours.

ICE CREAM

FRUIT SORBETS AND ICE CREAMS

Coconut Milk and Raspberry Ice Cream

Preparation time + freezing for ideal consumption: 5-6 hours

Ingredients for 4-6

250g / 9 oz / 1 ⅔ cups fresh raspberries

juice and zest of 1 unwaxed lime

400 ml / 14 fl. oz / 1 ⅔ cups coconut milk

100 g / 3 ½ oz / ½ cup sugar

50 ml / 1 ¾ fl. oz / ¼ cup agave syrup

Wash the raspberries and cover with lime juice.

Pour the coconut milk, one pack of raspberries, the sugar, syrup and lime zest into a large bowl. With a stick blender, cream the mixture, pour it into the ice cream/sorbet maker and follow the instructions.

Before pouring the mixture into the freezer container, add the remaining whole raspberries. If you are not using an ice cream maker, whip thoroughly and pour into a suitable container, then place it in the freezer.

After an hour, whip again and place it in the freezer. After another hour, check that lumps have not formed. If so, use a stick blender for a final whisking.

Lastly, add the whole raspberries and leave to chill in the freezer.

Instead of raspberries, you could also use pineapple or strawberries without changing the weights and method.

Watermelon and Raspberry Frappé

Preparation time: 10 minutes

Ingredients for 4

2 slices watermelon

5 scoops vanilla ice cream

125 g / 4 ⅓ oz / ¾ cup fresh raspberries

¼ tsp ground cardamom

4 cubes white chocolate

Clean the watermelon, removing the rind and seeds.

Whizz in a blender with the ice cream.

Add half of the raspberries, washed and chopped in half, and the cardamom.

Mix and pour into glasses. Decorate with the remaining whole raspberries and a grating of white chocolate. Serve immediately.

Strawberry and Basil Sorbet

Preparation time + freezing for ideal consumption: 5-6 hours

Ingredients for 4-6

155 g / 5 ⅓ oz / ⅔ cup sugar

pinch of fleur de sel

65 g / 2 ⅓ fl. oz / ⅓ cup glucose syrup

125 ml / 4 ⅓ fl. oz / ½ cup water

handful of basil leaves

500 g / 17 ⅔ oz / 3 ⅓ cups hulled strawberries

1 tsp balsamic vinegar

In small pan, make a hot infusion with the sugar, fleur de sel, glucose syrup, water and basil leaves. As soon as it comes to the boil, check that the sugar has melted, turn off the heat and leave to cool. Filter to remove the basil leaves.

In the meantime, blend the strawberries. Pass through a fine sieve and mix with the prepared syrup. Lastly, add the balsamic vinegar.

Place in the freezer for at least an hour, then blend the mixture using a stick blender and place back in the freezer for another hour; repeat this process one more time the next hour.

Chill the sorbet in the freezer for 4 hours. Serve in scoops, decorated with a basil leaf. Naturally, if you have a sorbet maker, you can use it following the manufacturer's instructions.

Strawberry and Cherry Red Ice Cream

Serve in a cone or in a cup with banana and slices of strawberry.

Preparation time + freezing for ideal consumption: 5-6 hours

Ingredients for 4-6

180 ml / 6 ⅓ fl. oz / ⅔ cup oat milk

2 g carob seed flour

300 g / 10 ½ oz / 2 cups strawberry flesh

200 g / 7 oz / 1 ⅔ cups cherry flesh

juice of 1 lemon

100 g / 3 ½ oz / ½ cup raw cane sugar

It is important that the fruit is ripened to perfection and is not bruised. Warm the milk a little and dissolve the carob flour. Chop both fruits into chunks and sprinkle immediately with the lemon juice.

Place them in the blender bowl and blend with the sugar and milk, also adding the cooled milk with the carob flour until you get a fluid cream.

Pour the mixture into an ice cream/sorbet maker and follow the instructions. If you are not using an ice cream maker, beat and place in a suitable container, then place in the freezer. After an hour, beat again and place it back in the freezer. After another hour, check that no lumps have formed. If so, use a stick blender for the last beating.

Strawberry Frappé

Preparation time: 10 minutes

Ingredients for 2

125g / 4 ⅓ oz / ¾ cup fresh strawberries

1 tsp icing sugar (confectioner's sugar)

4 scoops strawberry ice cream

200 ml / 6 ¾ fl. oz / 2 cups whole creamy yogurt

handful fresh mint

Wash and hull the strawberries and chop them into chunks.

Sprinkle them with the sugar, mix and then place them in the stick blender beaker (reserving a couple of spoonfuls to use for decoration). Add the ice cream and yogurt and blend. You will get a dense and fragrant cream.

Divide it into two glasses and decorate the top with the remaining strawberries and the fresh mint.

Berry Frappé

You can create infinite variations of this recipe using mixed berries, blueberries, blackberries, strawberries or blackcurrants.

Preparation time: 10 minutes

Ingredients for 2

200 g / 7 oz / 2 cups mulberries (or blackberries)

2 tbsp icing sugar (confectioner's sugar)

juice of 1 lemon

2 scoops of blueberry ice cream (see basic ice cream recipes in Preparation chapter)

2 scoops of white ice cream (see basic ice cream recipe in Preparation chapter)

Clean and wash the mulberries, place them in a bowl and sprinkle with the sugar and lemon juice.

After a few minutes add the ice creams and, with a stick blender, blend until creamy.

Pour into tall glasses and serve with a straw.

You can choose to use a different fruit, yogurt, or combine yogurt and fresh milk.

Soy Yogurt and Blueberry Ice Cream

These little ice creams are very simple and are perfect for an afternoon snack. There are infinite variations; all you need is a plain vegan yogurt - ideally a very creamy one - and add whatever fruit you like.

Preparation time + freezing for ideal consumption: 5-6 hours

Ingredients for 4-6

150 g / 5 oz / 1 cup fresh blueberries

1 tsp vanilla extract

500 g / 17 ⅔ oz / 2 cups blueberry soy yogurt

Wash the blueberries in cold water, pour them into a bowl and sprinkle them with the vanilla extract.

Mix and add all the yogurt to the fresh blueberries.

Pour into the moulds – ideally silicon moulds – and place directly in the freezer for at least 5 hours.

Berry and White Chocolate Ice Cream

This ice cream bar is packed with nutritious fruit. You can also make this, like other ice creams, in an ice cream maker and serve it in a cone. In any case, it will be much appreciated as an afternoon snack.

Preparation time + freezing for ideal consumption: 5-6 hours

Ingredients for 4-6

150g / 5 oz / 1 cup fresh blackberries

150g / 5 oz / 1 cup fresh blueberries

4 squares white chocolate (plus 4 more for decoration)

250 g / 9 oz / 1 cup creamy plain yogurt

50 g / 1 ¾ oz / ¼ cup caster (superfine) sugar

Wash the blackberries and blueberries thoroughly and place them in the blender beaker with 4 squares of white chocolate. Blend for a moment.

Add the yogurt and sugar, then blend again until you have a velvety, creamy sauce. If it seems too dense, dilute it with a few spoons of cool whole milk. Taste to check that the flavour and, above all, the amount of sugar is to your taste.

Pour into your chosen moulds and place in the freezer for a few hours, ideally overnight. If you like, once you have taken the ice creams out of the moulds, put them on a plate and decorate by drizzling with white chocolate, melted in the microwave or over a bain-marie.

Put them back in the freezer for 5 minutes before serving.

Kiwi and Mint Ice Cream

A very delicately flavoured ice cream that children will love. You could also serve it in a cone, between two wafers or with a fresh fruit salad.

Preparation time + freezing for ideal consumption: 5-6 hours

Ingredients for 4-6

8 kiwis

juice and zest of 2 unwaxed limes

4 tbsp creamy plain yogurt

4 tbsp granulated sugar

2 sprigs fresh mint

Peel the kiwis, chop them into cubes and place them in the stick blender beaker. Add the lime zest (the green part only), lime juice and mint. Leave to absorb the flavour for at least an hour.

Remove the mint, add the sugar and yogurt. Blend until you have a very soft, fluffy purée.

Pour the mixture into ice cream moulds, ideally silicon moulds, or place in the ice cream/sorbet maker and follow the instructions.

If you are whipping by hand, use the planetary mixer with the whisk to whip the entire mixture for a few minutes (it will increase in volume a bit), then pour it into a large container, place it in the freezer for an hour, then beat it and place it back in the freezer. Repeat this process twice more.

Apple and Ginger Sorbet

This really is a classic taste. Serve this sorbet in a cone or in a cup, adding slices of apple.

Preparation time + freezing for ideal consumption: 5-6 hours

Ingredients for 4-6

400 g / 14 oz / 2 ⅔ cups apples

500 ml / 17 ⅔ fl. oz / 2 cups water

180 g / 6 ⅓ oz / ¾ cup sugar

1 egg white

juice and zest of 1 unwaxed lemon

2 cm fresh ginger

In a small pan, simmer the water, sugar and lemon zest on a low heat for a few minutes. Then turn off and remove from the heat, grate the ginger directly into the syrup and leave to cool.

Wash the apples well but do not peel them.

Cut them into wedges and remove their cores and seeds. Chop them into cubes and, with a stick blender, blend them with the lemon juice and the filtered syrup until creamy.

Pour the mixture into a wide, shallow container and place in the freezer for at least another hour.

Blend the mixture with a stick blender and place it back in the freezer for an hour. Repeat the process once more after 40 minutes. Chill the sorbet in the freezer for at least 2 hours.

Once the time is up, whip the egg white into stiff peaks and gently add it to the sorbet, mixing with a whisk in an upward motion so as to avoid deflating it. Place the mixture back in the freezer for an hour.

Serve accompanied with freshly sliced apple.

Orange Spritz Iced Cocktail

This is not suitable for children but could cheer up your summer drinks and cocktails. A version for children or those that do not enjoy alcohol can be created by using blood orange juice and water in equal parts.

Preparation time + freezing for ideal consumption: 5-6 hours

Ingredients for 4-6

200 ml / 6 ¾ fl. oz / 1 cup water

100 ml / 3 ½ fl. oz / ½ cup prosecco

75 ml / 2 ⅔ fl. oz / ⅓ cup orange juice

75 ml / 2 ⅔ fl. oz / ⅓ cup Aperol

60 g / 2 ¼ oz / ¼ cup sugar

30 ml glucose syrup

20 g inulin (optional)

Heat the water without bringing it to the boil and dissolve the sugar and glucose.

Leave it to cool, then add all the other ingredients and mix with a stick blender.

Pour into the ice cream/sorbet maker and follow the instructions. If you are continuing manually, whisk thoroughly and pour into a suitable container, then place in the freezer. After an hour, beat again and put it back in the freezer. After another hour, check that lumps have not formed. If so, use a stick blender for a final whisking. Finally, leave to chill in the freezer.

Piña Colada Iced Cocktail

Preparation time: 5 minutes

Ingredients for 4

100 ml / 3 ½ fl. oz / ½ cup (dense) coconut milk

2 cups crushed ice

6 scoops pineapple ice cream

50 ml / 1 ¾ fl. oz / ¼ cup fresh cream

50 ml / 1 ¾ fl. oz / ¼ cup rum

Place all the ingredients in the blender beaker and mix at the highest speed for a few minutes.

Pour the cream you obtain into glasses and decorate to taste with grated lime zest and coconut flakes.

This one is alcoholic - not suitable for children!

VEGAN

Pear and Almond Milk Ice Cream

Preparation time + freezing for ideal consumption: 5-6 hours

Ingredients for 4-6

300 ml / 10 fl. oz / 1 ¼ cups almond milk

200 g / 7 oz / 1 ⅔ cups pear flesh

200 ml / 6 ¾ fl. oz / 1 cup plant cream (rice or oat)

85 g / 3 oz / ⅓ cup raw cane sugar

50 g / 1 ¾ oz / ¼ cup agave syrup

1 tbsp almonds, finely chopped

Chop the pears into cubes, place in a small pan and cover with half of the almond milk. Bring to the boil, add the sugar, mix for a couple of minutes, then turn out and leave to cool completely.

Add all of the other ingredients to the mixture (except the almonds) and with a stick blender, blend until you have a soft cream.

Pour into a freezer container and place in the freezer immediately. After an hour, blend again, repeat this process twice more.

Serve sprinkled with the chopped almonds, lightly toasted.

You can also serve this ice cream inside a pear: hollow out the pear keeping 0.5 cm of flesh attached to the skin, trying to avoid it breaking. Sprinkle lemon juice into the pear before placing the ice cream inside, in order to avoid the pear burning brown.

Yellow Pear Sorbet

Preparation time + freezing for ideal consumption: 5-6 hours

Ingredients for 4-6

500 g / 17 ⅔ oz / 4 cups ripe pear flesh

130 g / 4 ½ oz / ½ cup raw cane sugar

50 g / 1 ¾ oz / ¼ cup agave syrup

juice of 2 lemons

1 tsp saffron

Chop the pears into cubes, place in a small pan, cover with the sugar and lemon juice, add the saffron and agave syrup, just cover with water and bring to the boil.

Mix well, turn off the heat and leave to cool. Blend until you have a smooth, soft mixture with no lumps.

Pour into the ice cream/sorbet maker and follow the instructions.

If you are continuing by hand, beat thoroughly and pour into a suitable container, then place in the freezer. After an hour, beat again and put it back in the freezer. After another hour, check that lumps have not formed. If so, use a stick blender for a final whisking. Finally, leave to cool.

di quelli
nascesse
ascoltando
con il
immaginò che
di una
perderemo
sempre molto meno di
a conquistare.

Classic Orange Lollies

Bright, cheerful and packed with vitamins.

Preparation time + freezing for ideal consumption: 5-6 hours

Ingredients for 4-6

50 g / 1 ¾ oz / ¼ cup sugar

50 ml / 1 ¾ fl. oz / ¼ cup water

grated zest of 2 mandarins

300 g / 10 ⅔ oz / 2 ½ cups mango flesh

200 ml / 7 fl. oz / 1 cup mandarin juice

2 cm fresh ginger, chopped

In a small pan, dissolve the sugar in the water bringing it to the boil for a moment. Turn off the heat and add the mandarin zest.

When it has cooled completely, filter the syrup and add it to the mango chopped into chunks, mandarin juice and ginger in the blender bowl.

Blend until you have a smooth purée and pour into the ice cream or ice lolly moulds. Keep them in the freezer overnight for best results.

Alternatively, pour the mixture into the ice cream/sorbet maker using the sorbet programme.

Limoncello Lollies

Preparation time + freezing for ideal consumption: 8 hours

Ingredients for 4-6

300 ml / 10 fl. oz / 1 ¼ cups water

100 g / 3 ½ oz / ½ cup sugar

50 ml / 1 ¾ fl. oz / ¼ cup limoncello

200 ml / 6 ¾ fl. oz / 1 cup lemon juice

grated zest of 1 unwaxed lemon

In a saucepan, combine the water and sugar over a low heat. Heat until the sugar has dissolved.

Add the water, lemon juice and zest and leave to cool at room temperature. Lastly, add the limoncello.

Mix and pour into ice lolly moulds. You will end up with a sorbet lolly. Alternatively, follow the same method as for other sorbets – if possible use an ice cream maker or beat once an hour for at least four hours.

Serve by the spoon in cups or glasses.

VEGAN

Pink Grapefruit Sorbet

This sorbet is great served with vodka and pomegranate juice. It also looks brilliant if you serve it inside the grapefruit itself.

Preparation time + freezing for ideal consumption: 5-6 hours

Ingredients for 4-6

350 ml / 12 ⅓ fl. oz / 1 ½ cups filtered pink grapefruit juice

100 g / 3 ½ oz / ½ cup sugar

50 ml / 1 ¾ fl. oz / ¼ cup agave syrup

200 ml / 6 ¾ fl. oz / 1 cup water

Place the sugar, syrup and water in a small pan. Bring to the boil, leaving to simmer for a couple of minutes, then turn off the heat and leave to cool.

Add the grapefruit juice and mix well to blend the liquids.

Pour into the ice cream/sorbet maker and follow the instruction. If you are not using an ice cream maker, beat thoroughly and pour into a suitable container, then place in the freezer.

After an hour, beat again and place back in the freezer. After another hour, check that lumps have not formed. If so, use a stick blender for a final whisking. Finally, leave to chill in the freezer.

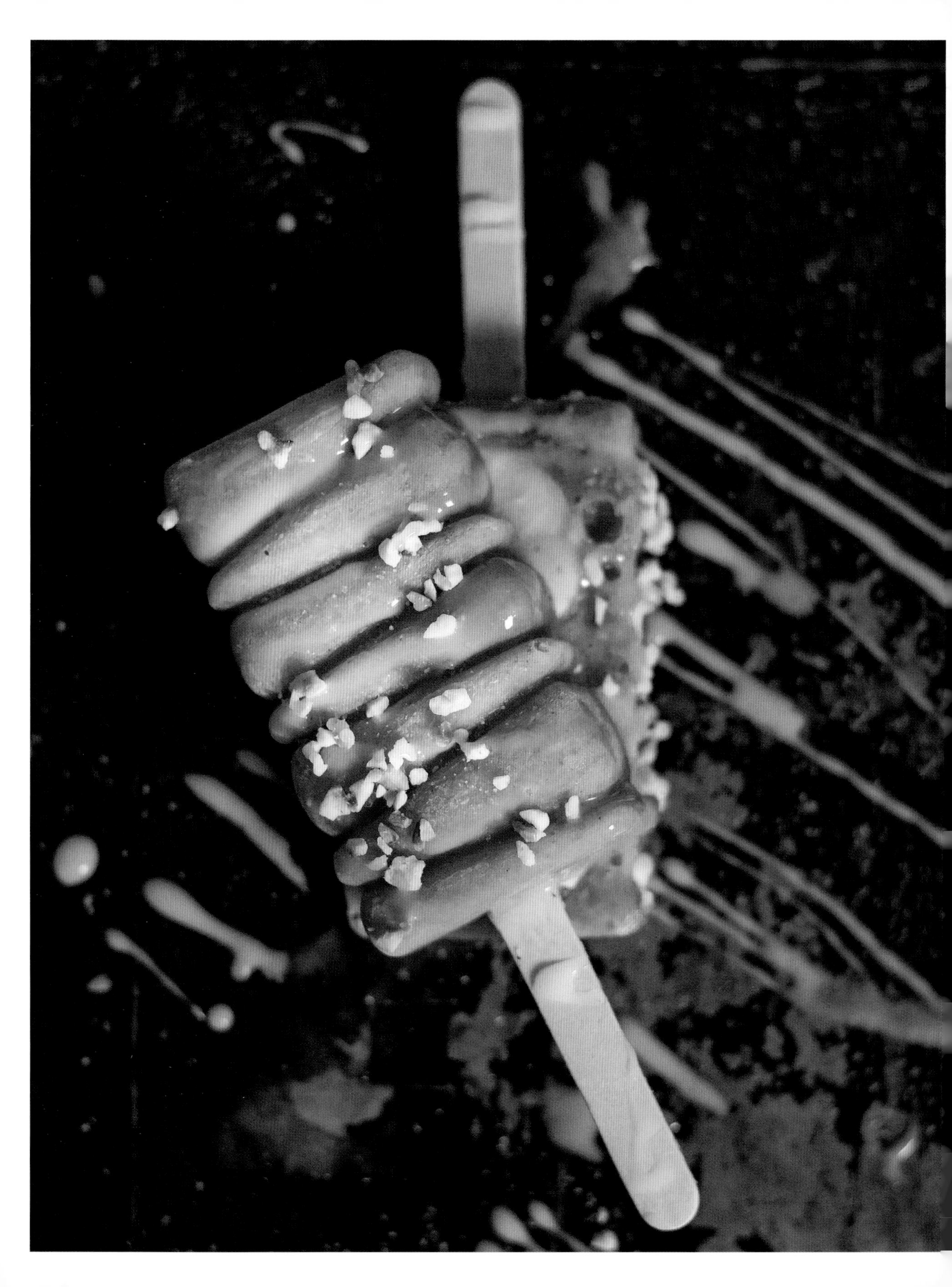

Spiced Banana Lollies

Preparation time + freezing for ideal consumption: 5-6 hours

Ingredients for 4-6

400 g / 14 oz / 3 ¼ cups banana flesh (+ 1 banana for decoration)

220 ml / 7 ½ fl. oz / ¾ cup rice milk

50 g / 1 ¾ oz / ¼ cup raw cane sugar

juice of 1 lemon

1 tsp ground spices (ginger, anise, pepper, cinnamon, coriander seed)

To ensure you get tasty ice cream, it is important that the bananas are ripened to perfection and not bruised. Slice the bananas and immediately cover with the lemon juice so they do not blacken.

Place in the blender bowl and beat with the sugar, milk and spices until you get a fluid cream.

At this point, you can choose whether to pour the mixture into the ice cream/sorbet maker and follow the instructions, or to use ice cream moulds and place it directly in the freezer.

If you go for the second option, when you pour the ice cream into the container, add a sliced banana and stir it in. Finding the little pieces of fruit will be a real treat!

To make the ice cream more creamy, you can add a teaspoon of carob seed flour (this applies to all the ice creams that do not involve the use of cow's milk and cream).

Sweet Coconut Lollies

Preparation time + freezing for ideal consumption: 5-6 hours

Ingredients for 4-6

350 g / 12 oz / 1 ½ cups whole milk

150 g / 5 oz / ⅔ cup coconut milk

50 g / 1 ¾ oz / ½ cup dessicated coconut

100 g / 3 ½ oz / ½ cup sugar

200 g / 7 oz / 1 ⅓ cups dark chocolate with 75 per cent cocoa (optional)

Warm the whole milk. Pour the dessicated coconut and sugar into a bowl, cover with the warmed milk and leave to rest until the mixture cools, stirring from time to time and checking that the sugar dissolves completely.

Once the mixture has cooled, add the coconut milk and beat with a hand whisk to remove any lumps and lightly aerate the mixture.

Pour into the ice cream/sorbet maker and follow the instructions. When the ice cream is ready, but still soft, pour it directly into the moulds (or little glasses). If you are not using an ice cream maker, pour the mixture into the planetary mixer bowl and beat for a few minutes. Then freeze and repeat the whipping process with a hand whisk after an hour. Lastly, pour into the moulds.

When the ice cream is well frozen (preferably the day after preparation), melt the chocolate over a bain-marie.

Once the chocolate is runny, mix it again to cool it slightly and rapidly immerse the ice creams in it, then place them back in the freezer immediately.

Alternatively, rest them on greaseproof paper and quickly decorate them with the chocolate and dust with coconut flakes. Or, take care not to fill the moulds completely with the ice cream and leave space to drizzle in the chocolate when the ice creams are frozen to create a crunchy base all along the side.

Cinnamon and Apple Ice Cream

Preparation time + freezing for ideal consumption: 5-6 hours

Ingredients for 4-6

225 ml / 8 fl. oz / 1 cup fresh cream

280 ml / 9 ¾ fl. oz / 1 ¼ cups whole milk

300 g / 10 ½ oz / 2 ½ cups apple flesh

130 g / 4 ½ oz / ½ cup light cane sugar

½ tsp ground cinnamon

1 vanilla pod (seeds only)

juice of ½ lemon

2 cloves

Chop the apple into cubes, cover with the lemon juice, sprinkle with the sugar and simmer in a small pan over a very low heat. The apple will release its juices and caramelise slightly.

Leave it to cool a little then blend, if necessary, adding a tiny drop of milk.

In the meantime, warm the cream with the cloves, vanilla seeds and cinnamon. Bring almost to the boil and the turn off the heat. Leave to rest until it has cooled completely.

In the planetary mixer, add the blended apple, milk and sieved cream, beat together with the whisk and pour into the ice cream/sorbet maker.

Follow the instructions, the pour the ice cream into a freezer container and chill until frozen. This ice cream requires beating in the ice cream maker for best results.

Serve it in scoops with a slice of apple pie - it will really bring out the flavour.

Chestnut and Vanilla Ice Cream

Preparation time + freezing for ideal consumption: 5-6 hours

Ingredients for 4-6

200 g / 7 oz / 1 ⅔ cups boiled chestnuts

50 g / 1 ¾ oz / ¼ cup chestnut spread

220 ml / 7 ½ fl. oz / 1 cup fresh cream

150 ml / 5 ⅓ fl. oz / ⅔ cup whole milk

100 g / 3 ½ oz / ½ cup light raw cane sugar

1 tsp natural vanilla extract

Place the roughly crumbled chestnuts, chestnut spread, the vanilla extract, sugar and milk in a small saucepan.

Bring to the boil, then turn off the heat. Leave to cool and blend until you get a smooth purée with no lumps.

Fold in the lightly whipped cream and if you are using an ice cream maker, follow the instructions. If you are continuing by hand, beat thoroughly and pour into a suitable container, then place in the freezer.

After an hour, beat again and put it back in the freezer. After another hour, check that lumps have not formed. If they have, use a stick blender for the final beating. Finally, leave to chill until frozen.

With an ice cream scoop, serve two scoops per person.

You can decorate the ice cream with a dollop of cream, dark chocolate shavings, caramel or a few chestnuts that you have caramelised in advance.

DAIRY ICE CREAM, FROZEN YOGURT AND CHOCOLATE

Crème Fraîche Ice Cream

Preparation time + freezing for ideal consumption: 5-6 hours

Ingredients for 4-6

225 g / 8 oz / ¾ cup traditional Greek yogurt

100 g / 3 ½ oz / ½ cup crème fraîche

150 ml / 5 ⅓ fl. oz / ⅔ cup whole milk

100 g / 3 ½ oz / ½ cup sugar

Mix together all of the ingredients with an electric (or hand) whisk, pour them into the ice cream/sorbet maker and set the time.

Once the ice cream is ready, keep it in the freezer. If you are not using an ice cream maker, beat as in the previous recipes. Serve to taste with saffron honey.

VARIATIONS

- Leave out the crème fraîche and increase the milk to 195 ml.
- Add chopped fruit to the ice cream.
- Replace the sugar with 40 g / 1 ⅓ oz / ¼ cup of acacia honey.

Ripples

You can ripple the yogurt with fruit sauces or chocolate creams (such as the famous hazelnut cream).

Fruity Sauce

Preparation time: 5 minutes

For 300 g of sauce

160 g / 5 ⅔ oz / 1 ¼ cups fruit (such as raspberries or strawberries)

35 g sugar

65 g / 2 ¼ oz / ⅓ cup glucose syrup

25 g honey

15 ml lemon juice

Warm and dissolve all of the sugars in the lemon juice. Do not bring to the boil: you should end up with a transparent syrup.

Leave to cool, stirring from time to time.

Clean, wash and blend the fruit with a mixer, then add it to the syrup. In this way, the sauce will not undergo changes in temperature and will be perfect for creating a ripple in the yogurt ice cream.

Raisin, Rum and Plant Milk Ice Cream

Preparation time + freezing for ideal consumption: 5-6 hours

Ingredients for 4

200 ml / 7 fl. oz / 1 cup vanilla-flavoured plant milk

200 g / 7 oz / ¾ cup plant cream

80 g / 2 ¾ oz / ⅓ cup raw cane sugar

1 g carob seed flour

2 tbsp sultanas

230 ml / 8 fl. oz / 1 cup brandy or rum

Place the sultanas to soak in the spirits.

Gently heat the milk, dissolve the sugar and carob flour and leave to cool. When it has cooled, add the plant cream.

Drain the sultanas, filter the spirits and add it to the mixture. Pour the mixture into the ice cream/ sorbet maker and follow the instructions.

When the ice cream becomes more dense, add the sultanas. If you are not using an ice cream maker, beat with a whisk, pour into a suitable container and then place in the freezer.

After an hour, beat again and place back in the freezer. The third time, add the sultanas and finish freezing.

This is a classic flavour that is hard to find in a vegan version.

Camera di Co

NEW YORK ARTE

Classic Vanilla Cups

Preparation time 10 minutes

Ingredients for 4-6

4 scoops vanilla ice cream (see basic ice cream recipes in Preparation chapter)

2 tbsp sultanas

4 crunchy chocolate biscuits

480 ml / 17 fl. oz / 2 cups rum

100 ml / 3 ½ fl. oz / ½ cup fresh cream, lightly whipped

Place the sultanas in the rum to soak for 5 minutes, then squeeze them out and remove, filter the rum and leave it to one side.

Crumble the biscuits into the base of two glasses or ice cream cups, or pour in a spoonful of Nocciolini.

Place two scoops of ice cream on top and half of the sultanas.

Drizzle with the rum, cover with a couple of spoons of soft cream and finish with the remaining sultanas.

If you like, you can grate some cocoa beans, which add a touch of bitterness, or some 75 per cent cocoa dark chocolate.

Triple Yogurt Ice Cream

This ice cream is quick to make when you don't have much time to spend too long in the kitchen. Naturally, the flavours and the colour combinations can be varied to suit your taste. Use low-fat yogurt for a lighter ice cream or full fat and with lots of different colours if you are making it for children.

Preparation time + cooling for ideal consumption: 12 hours

Ingredients for 4-6

200 g / 7 oz / ¾ cup strawberry yogurt

200 g / 7 oz / ¾ cup blueberry yogurt

200 g / 7 oz / ¾ cup creamy plain yogurt

Divide the strawberry yogurt between the moulds and place them in the freezer for an hour.

Add a layer of plain yogurt and repeat.

Finally, add the third layer using the blueberry yogurt. Then leave in the freezer overnight, so that all three layers freeze well.

Spicy Honey Ice Cream

Preparation time: 10 minutes

Ingredients for 4

500 ml / 17 ⅔ fl. oz / 2 cups plain yogurt ice cream (cow's milk or soy)

200 g / 7 oz / 1 ⅓ ice cubes

5 tbsp acacia honey

a pinch of ground nutmeg

a pinch of ground cinnamon

grated zest of 1 unwaxed lemon

Place all the ingredients in the mixer or stick blender beaker and blend at the highest speed until you obtain a dense and silky cream.

Divide into four glasses and dust with a grating of nutmeg.

Ice cream with Panettone

Preparation time + freezing for ideal consumption: 5-6 hours

Ingredients for 4-6

3 slices of toasted panettone, blended into flour + panettone to serve

160 ml / 5 ⅔ fl. oz / ⅔ cup fresh cream

340 ml / 12 fl. oz / 1 ½ cups fresh milk

150 ml / 5 ¼ fl. oz / ⅔ cup condensed milk

480 ml / 16 ¼ fl. oz / 2 cups orange liqueur

30 g sultanas

Rehydrate the sultanas by placing them in a bowl and soaking with a small glass of liqueur.

Pour the condensed milk, fresh milk and cream into the planetary mixer and begin to beat with the whisk at the highest speed.

Add the toasted panettone, one spoonful at a time, having previously blended into flour in the mixer. You will need about 4 tablespoons of flour – then the remaining liqueur. When the mixture is light, fluffy and firm, add the sultanas.

Transfer the mixture to the ice cream/sorbet maker and beat according to the instructions. Alternatively, place directly in the freezer with two options, manual beating or a much faster method: pour the ice cream into a loaf tin and leave to freeze without touching it again.
Serve it in slices, together with cubes of crunchy panettone.

To make the panettone crunchy, cut it into cubes and fry it in a pan lightly greased with butter. Turn it on all sides to turn it golden evenly.
If you want, you could even cut 1 cm (½ in) thick slices of panettone and fill with ice cream between two slices, making a sort of panettone ice cream sandwich. Place in the freezer for 10 minutes then cut in half and serve.

Dulce de Leche

Preparation time + freezing for ideal consumption: 6-8 hours

Ingredients for 4-6

FOR THE DULCE DE LECHE

500 ml / 17 fl. oz / 2 cups fresh whole milk

100 g / 3 ½ oz / ½ cup sugar

¼ tsp bicarbonate of soda (baking soda)

seeds of 1 vanilla pod

FOR THE ICE CREAM

200 g / 7 oz / ¾ cup dulce de leche

350 ml / 12 ⅓ fl. oz / 1 ½ cups whole milk

160 ml / 5 ⅔ fl. oz / ⅔ cup fresh cream

90 g / 3 ¼ oz / ½ cup sugar

FOR THE DULCE DE LECHE
Pour the milk, sugar and vanilla seeds into a deep saucepan. Bring to the boil.

When it begins to simmer, quickly add the bicarbonate, turning the heat to the minimum. The milk will rise up and make a lot of foam (hence the need for the deep saucepan).
You will need to keep an eye on it for the first half hour until the foam has reduced and the low simmering allows you to mix it only every now and again. The milk will slowly evaporate.

You will realise that the dulce is ready when you can see the bottom of the pan when you stir it. The milk will have turned into a soft caramel-coloured spread. Place it in a jar while it is still very hot and seal it hermetically. The alternative, which is certainly more convenient but also sweeter, is to put a sealed tin of condensed milk to boil in a saucepan of water for at least three hours. The water must cover the tin at all times and only simmer gently. It must also cool in water. When the tin has cooled completely, open and use according to the recipe.

FOR THE ICE CREAM
Pour all of the ingredients into the planetary mixer and activate the whisk at the highest speed. The mixture will become light and fluffy. Transfer it to your ice cream/sorbet maker and follow the instructions. If you are not using an ice cream maker, pour into a suitable container and beat with a whisk (ideally an electric one) every hour for at least three hours.

This is a very sweet ice cream. You could add dark chocolate shavings on serving.

Lavender and Rosemary Lollies

Preparation time + freezing for ideal consumption: 12 hours

Ingredients for 4-6

1 tbsp edible dried lavender

3 sprigs rosemary

150 ml / 5 ¼ fl. oz / ⅔ cup fresh cream

500 ml / 17 ⅔ fl. oz / 2 cups fresh whole milk

250 g / 8 ¾ oz / 1 cup condensed milk

3 tbsp lavender honey

fresh lavender and rosemary flowers (optional)

Place the dried lavender flowers together with 2 very fresh sprigs of rosemary in the cream to infuse overnight. Cover with cling film and leave in the fridge.

The next day, filter and pour the scented cream, whole milk, condensed milk and lavender honey into the planetary mixer. Activate the whisk at the maximum speed, whipping until the mixture is soft and frothy.

As the last ingredient, add the remaining rosemary leaves, finely chopped.

Pour into a freezer-proof container.

Beat again after an hour, then leave it to freeze in lolly moulds for a few hours.

Alternatively, leave the mixture to freeze before serving the ice cream in glasses, decorating it with lavender and rosemary and drizzling with honey to taste.

When beaten with a whisk, the mixture turns into a very soft and fluffy mousse, which may be served after just 20 minutes in the freezer.

Vanilla Ice Cream

Vanilla ice cream is a timeless classic. It can be combined with many other flavours and, if prepared with excellent ingredients, it is perfect served without accompaniment.

Preparation time + freezing for ideal consumption: 5-6 hours

Ingredients for 4-6

115 g / 4 oz / ½ cup fresh cream

2 Bourbon vanilla pods

465 g / 16 oz / 2 cups fresh whole milk

130 g / 4 ⅔ oz / ½ cup sugar

4 medium egg yolks

1 tsp of vanilla extract

In a small pan, heat the cream and vanilla pods, having extracted the seeds and placed them in liquid.

In a planetary mixer, using the whisk, beat the egg yolks with the sugar until the mixture is fluffy. Filter the milk and cream mixture and add the milk mixture to the egg and sugar mixture, a little at a time.

Beat with the whisk and transfer the ingredients back to the pan. Simmer over a low heat to create a custard. When it coats the back of the spoon (at 83–85°C/180F) remove from the heat and continue to stir to lower the temperature.

When the custard has cooled completely, add the vanilla extract and place in the ice cream/sorbet maker. Activate and follow the instructions.

Custard Ice Cream

Excellent as a base ice cream and perfect to accompany cakes or fruit.

Preparation time + freezing for ideal consumption: 5-6 hours

Ingredients for 4-6

6 egg yolks

150 g / 5 ¼ oz / ⅔ cup sugar

160 ml / 5 ⅔ fl. oz / ⅔ cup cream

440 ml / 15 ½ fl. oz / 1 ¾ cups milk

grated zest of 2 unwaxed lemons

3 tbsp pine nuts, lightly toasted

Beat the egg yolks and sugar with a whisk in the planetary mixer until you have a thick mixture. Meanwhile, heat the cream until it comes to the boil.

Turn off the heat, stir to lower the temperature and pour the mixture into the egg yolks in a steady trickle with the whisk running. Add the milk.

Beat well, pour the mixture into a saucepan together with the lemon zest and, stirring constantly with a wooden spoon, simmer at a very low heat until the custard coats the back of the spoon. Remove from the heat immediately and stir until it cools.

Finally, place the custard in the ice cream/sorbet maker and follow the instructions. Alternatively, if you are doing it manually, beat with an electric whisk (or planetary mixer) until the ice cream is the ideal consistency.

Spiced Coffee Ice Cream

Preparation time + cooling for ideal consumption: 5-6 hours

Ingredients for 4-6

250 ml / 8 ¾ fl. oz / 1 cup coffee

50 g / 1 ¾ oz / ½ cup dark chocolate

140 g / 5 oz / ⅔ cup sugar

20 g cocoa

½ tsp cinnamon

¼ tsp ground pink pepper

¼ tsp ground cardamom

2 cloves

200 ml / 7 fl. oz / ¾ cup fresh cream

100 ml / 3 ½ fl. oz / ⅓ cup whole milk

Prepare the coffee and finely chop the chocolate with a knife. Pour the coffee into a large bowl, melt the chocolate and sugar, then the cocoa and finally add the spices.

When it is cool, mix again, filter, place it in the planetary mixer (or use a whisk) and activate the whisk, adding the cream and milk.

Let it increase in volume slightly, then pour into the ice cream/sorbet maker and follow the instructions. If you are not using an ice cream maker, leave it in the planetary mixer for a few more minutes so that the cream is better aerated, then pour directly into a freezer container. Repeat the process with a whisk after an hour and a third time after another hour.

Serve the ice cream with fresh whipped cream dusted with cinnamon.

Experiment with the spices and choose those that are most to your taste.

Frozen Mocha

Preparation time: 10 minutes

Ingredients for 2

4 scoops coffee ice cream

1 pot of coffee

200 ml / 7 fl. oz / ¾ cup fresh cream, lightly whipped

Make some good, fairly strong coffee in the pot.

Place two scoops of ice cream in a glass, pour on the hot coffee and immediately add a good tablespoon of cream.

Serve immediately. If it suits your taste, add little grating of strong dark chocolate. If you like, prepare some good coffee the day before, put it in an ice tray and place it in the freezer overnight.

Place the iced coffee in the glass together with the scoops of ice cream, then add the semi-liquid cream and the hot coffee. Very spectacular and just as intense.

Spices that work well with coffee include cardamom, nutmeg, cloves, pink pepper, white pepper, red chilli, star anise, vanilla and ginger.

Soy Coffee Ice Cream

With this flavour, you can prepare a delicious affogato. Place a couple of scoops of ice cream in a large tall glass and cover with your preferred plant milk. As an alternative to soy milk, try vanilla-flavoured rice milk – its sweet, neutral flavour enhances the flavour of the coffee. You can also prepare ice creams on a stick and, when they are thoroughly frozen, quickly dip them in melted dark chocolate and then sprinkle them with finely chopped hazelnuts and put them back in the freezer for at least half an hour before eating.

Preparation time + cooling for ideal consumption: 5-6 hours

Ingredients for 4-6

350 ml / 12 ⅓ fl. oz / 1 ½ cups soy milk

150 ml / 5 ¼ fl. oz / ⅔ cup coffee or barley coffee

200 ml / 7 fl. oz / ¾ cup soy plant cream or creamed rice

140 g / 5 oz / ½ cup raw cane sugar

240 ml / 8 ½ fl. oz / 1 cup coffee liqueur (optional)

Make the coffee or barley coffee, add the sugar and stir immediately so that the sugar dissolves, then leave to cool completely.

Add the soy milk to the cooled coffee, beat with a whisk, then add the plant cream and whip.

Pour into an ice cream/sorbet maker and follow the instructions.

If you want to add coffee liqueur, do so just before pouring the mixture into the ice cream maker.

You can skip the ice cream maker stage if you want to prepare ice creams on sticks.

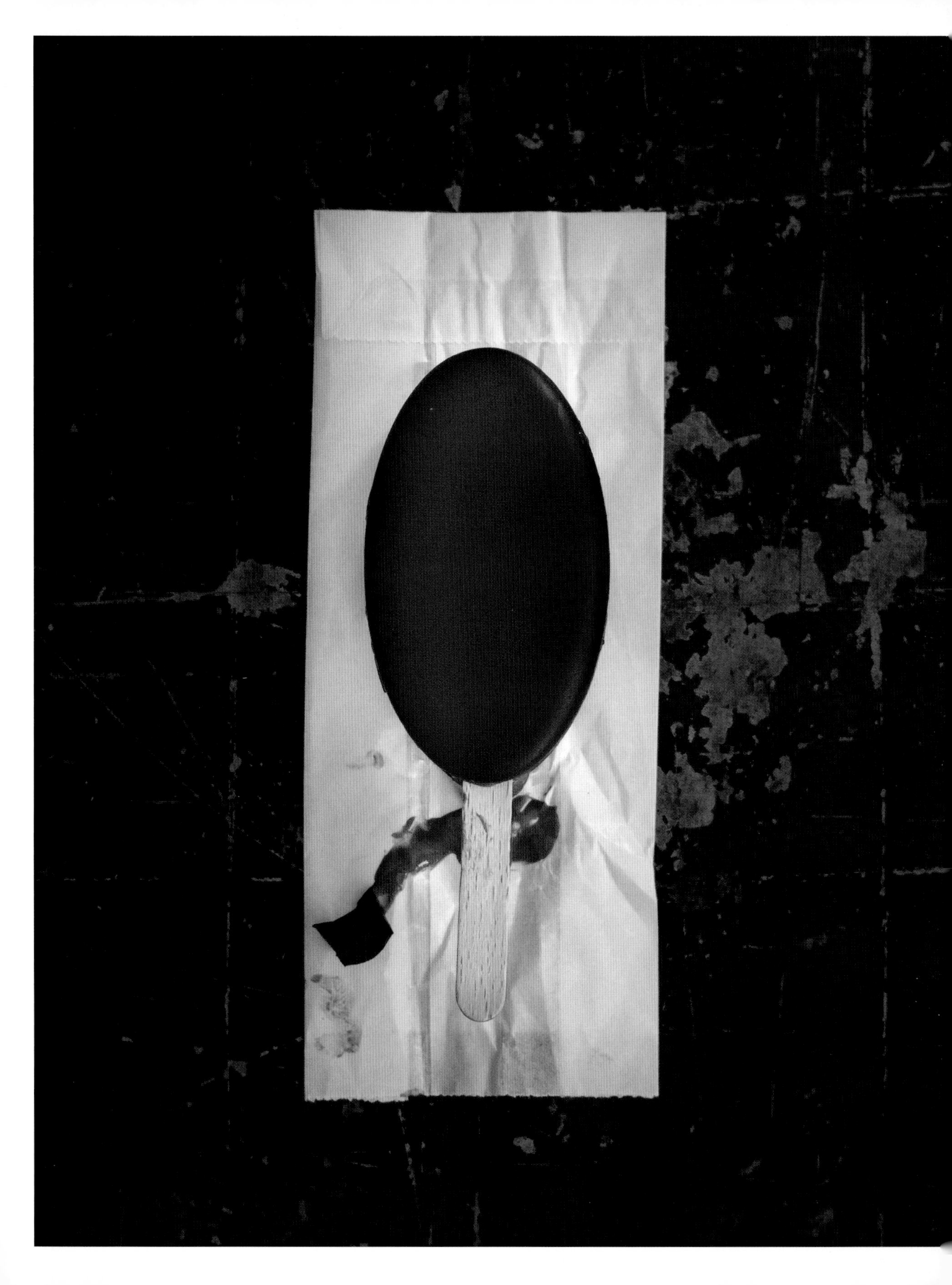

Dark Chocolate and Wasabi Sorbet

These ice creams are really tasty and different. Once they're frozen in the silicon moulds, they are removed and plunged into melted white or dark chocolate for a few seconds. They are then placed back in the freezer to freeze the chocolate onto the sorbet.

Preparation time + freezing for ideal consumption: 5-6 hours

Ingredients for 4-6

155 g / 5 ½ oz / 1 ¼ cups dark chocolate with 75 per cent cocoa

50 g / 1 ¾ oz / ½ cup cocoa

170 g / 6 oz / ¾ cup sugar

490 ml / 17 ¼ fl. oz / 2 cups water

2 g carob seed flour

¼ tsp wasabi paste or powder

Place the water in a large saucepan and bring to the boil. As soon as it comes to the boil, remove from the heat and add the cocoa and sugar, beating with a whisk.

Replace on the heat and leave to simmer for around 3 minutes.

Turn off the heat and add the chocolate, roughly broken into pieces, and the carob flour. Stir well to allow the chocolate to dissolve completely.

Leave to cool, stirring from time to time.

At this point, add the wasabi, pour the mixture into the ice cream/sorbet maker and follow the instructions. If you are not using an ice cream maker, beat thoroughly and pour into a suitable container, the place in the freezer.

After an hour, beat again and put it back in the freezer. After another hour, check that lumps have not formed. If so, use a stick blender for a final whisking. Finally, leave to cool.

If you prefer, you could choose a chocolate that is not so strong, but try not to go below 65 per cent cocoa content.

Pistachio, Rosebud and White Chocolate Ice Cream

Preparation time + freezing for ideal consumption: 5-6 hours

Ingredients for 4-6

335 ml / 11 ¾ fl. oz / 1 ½ cups whole milk

150 ml / 5 ¼ fl. oz / ⅔ cup fresh cream

150 g / 5 ¼ oz / 1 ¼ cups white chocolate

75 ml / 2 ⅔ oz / ½ cup condensed milk

80 g / 2 ¾ oz / ⅔ cup whole or crushed pistachios

2 tbsp edible rosebuds

Heat the milk and leave the rosebuds to infuse for at least one night. In a bowl, heat the white chocolate over a bain-marie and let it melt until it has liquified. If necessary, add some hot milk. Mix constantly, as white chocolate tends to form lumps and not be compact.

Once ready, pour the mixture into the planetary mixer and beat with the whisk, allowing it to cool slightly.

Add the filtered milk, condensed milk and cream. Leave the whisk running until the mixture is very light and fluffy.

At this point, pour the mixture into the ice cream/sorbet maker, which will finish the job. Add the pistachios when there are only a couple of minutes left until the end of beating.

If you are not using an ice cream maker, the tips provided in the preceding recipes apply. In this case too, add the pistachios as the last ingredient.

As an alternative to pistachios, try hazelnuts - they are excellent with white chocolate. In this case, leave out the rose scent and go for vanilla instead.

PRODUCT OF FRANCE
HARVESTED IN AIGUES-MORTES
Alban Mouret
MASTER SALT MAKER
FLEUR DE SE
R DE SEL

Chocolate, Fleur de Sel and Pink Pepper Ice Cream

These ice creams make a particularly tasty dessert or treat.

Preparation time + freezing for ideal consumption: 5-6 hours

Ingredients for 4-6

500 ml / 17 ⅔ fl. oz / 2 cups milk

100 g / 3 ½ oz / ½ cup sugar

100 g / 3 ½ oz / ¾ cup dark chocolate with 70 per cent cocoa

3 egg yolks (remember to use very fresh eggs)

2 tsp fleur de sel

1 tsp pink pepper

2 tbsp dark chocolate chips

In the planetary mixer, beat the egg yolks with the sugar until they are pale and frothy.

In the meantime, heat the milk, without bringing it to the boil, and add the egg yolks, a little at a time.

At this point, heat the chocolate over a bain-marie and, once melted, add it to the milk and egg mixture.

Before switching off the ice cream maker which, in the meantime, will have made the mixture light and fluffy, add the fleur de sel, a teaspoon at a time (so that you can taste the mixture and not overdo it) and the pink pepper, pre-crushed with a pestle and mortar.

Transfer to the ice cream/sorbet maker and follow the instructions. Before the ice cream has finished freezing, add the chocolate chips.

If you like, serve with a couple of grains of fleur de sel or dark chocolate broken with a knife.

For this ice cream, it is advisable to use an ice cream maker. Alternatively, hand beating must be performed at regular intervals.

Reverse Stracciatella Ice Cream

This stracciatella is exactly the opposite of the classic recipe, which is made with cream ice cream and pieces of dark chocolate. In this recipe, dark chocolate ice cream is produced and combined with white chocolate chips.

Preparation time + freezing for ideal consumption: 5-6 hours

Ingredients for 4-6

450 ml / 15 ¾ fl. oz / 1 ¾ cups whole milk

80 g /2 ¾ oz / ⅓ cup sugar

100 g / 3 ½ oz / ¾ cup dark chocolate with 65 per cent cocoa

4 egg yolks

200 g / 7 oz / 1 ⅔ cups white chocolate

In the planetary mixer beat the egg yolks with the sugar until they are frothy.

In the meantime, in a saucepan, melt the chocolate in the hot milk, stir to lower the temperature and then add the mixture to the eggs. Whisk well.

Place the mixture in the ice cream/sorbet maker and follow the instructions.

While the ice cream maker is running, carefully break up the white chocolate with a knife.

You could also use more convenient chocolate chips, if you like.

When the ice cream is almost ready, add the chocolate and pour into a freezer container.
As for the other ice creams, it is possible to beat them by hand.

milk
latte

chocolate

Milk and Chocolate Ice Cream

This is the milkshake that children like best. You can decorate the glass with fresh fruit or accompany it with a fruit salad for a delicious snack. You can also pour the mixture into ice cream or ice lolly moulds and leave them in the freezer overnight.

Preparation time: 10 minutes

Ingredients for 2

4 scoops of dark chocolate ice cream (see basic ice cream recipes in Preparation chapter)

150 ml / 5 ¼ fl. oz / ⅔ cup whole milk

150 ml / 5 ¼ fl. oz / ⅔ cup fresh single cream

1 tsp icing sugar

Place the dark chocolate ice cream in the stick blender beaker.

Add the milk, cream and sugar and blend at the highest speed.

Pour into the glasses and serve with a straw. For a lavish touch, add a dollop of cream.

Pistachio Ice Cream

Preparation time + freezing for ideal consumption: 12 hours

Ingredients for 4-6

100 ml / 3 ½ fl. oz / ⅓ cup cream
400 ml / 14 fl. oz / 1 ⅔ cups whole milk
3 egg yolks
135 g / 4 ¾ oz / ½ cup sugar
250 g / 8 ¾ oz / 2 cups pistachios, shelled
1 vanilla pod

Roughly chop 100 g / 3 ½ oz of pistachios and leave them to infuse in the cream overnight.

The next day, place the egg yolks and sugar in the planetary mixer bowl. Beat with the whisk, at high speed until you get a creamy, light and fluffy mixture.

Filter the cream and add it, pouring it into the egg mixture in a slow steady trickle with the whisk running.

Once it has blended well, pour the mixture into a saucepan and stirring constantly with a wooden spoon, simmer over a low heat.

When the custard coats the back of a spoon, remove from the heat immediately and mix until cool.

While you stir, add the pistachios that you previously infused in the cream, plus a further 100 g / 3 ½ oz, all finely chopped, or better still blended to a paste.

Lastly, put the custard in the ice cream/sorbet maker, add the vanilla seeds and follow the instructions.

Towards the end of beating, add the remaining pistachios, leaving them whole or breaking them with a knife. Alternatively, if you are doing it manually beat with an electric whisk (or using a planetary mixer) at least each hour in the freezer until the ice cream reaches the ideal consistency.

Mint Lollies with Dark Chocolate

Preparation time + freezing for ideal consumption: 12 hours

Ingredients for 4-6

400 ml / 14 fl. oz / 1 ⅔ cups whole milk

100 ml / 3 ½ fl. oz / 1 ½ cups full fat yogurt

100 ml / 3 ½ fl. oz / 1 ½ cups mint syrup

150 g / 5 ⅓ oz / 1 ½ cups dark chocolate with 70 per cent cocoa

Pour all of the ingredients, except the chocolate, into a large container, mix together and pour the mixture into ice lolly moulds or plastic cups.

Insert the wooden stick and leave in the freezer for a few hours.

When they are solid, quickly cover the base with a coating of melted chocolate, which will solidify immediately, or dip the tip of the ice cream in the melted chocolate, then immediately place it back in the freezer. Another option is to place them on greaseproof paper and with a fork or a little whisk, rapidly drizzle the chocolate over the ice creams in a wavy motion.

Leave to cool for a few minutes in the freezer before serving.

Ice Cream with Spices

Preparation time + freezing for ideal consumption: 5-6 hours

Ingredients for 4-6

100 ml / 3 ½ fl. oz / ½ cup cream

300 ml / 10 ½ fl. oz / 1 ¼ cups whole milk

6 egg yolks

135 g / 4 ¾ oz / ½ cup raw cane sugar

FOR THE SPICE MIX

seeds of ½ vanilla pod

½ tsp cinnamon

¼ tsp ground cloves

¼ tsp ground ginger

¼ tsp ground cardamom

¼ tsp pepper

VARIATIONS

- You can leave two black teabags to infuse in the cream the evening before preparation, then continue according to the recipe. This will make the ice cream will be even more aromatic.
- You can make the ice cream even more luxurious by serving it with soft caramel.

Place the egg yolks and sugar in the planetary mixer bowl.

Beat with the whisk, at high speed, until you get a creamy, light and fluffy mixture.

Add the milk to the egg mixture in a slow steady trickle, with the whisk running.

Once all the ingredients have blended well, pour the mixture into a saucepan and, stirring constantly with a wooden spoon, simmer over a very low heat.

As soon as the custard coats the back of the spoon, take it off the heat and stir until it cools.

In the meantime add the spice mix and lastly the cream.

Place the mixture in the ice cream/sorbet maker and follow the instructions. Alternatively, if you are doing it manually beat with an electric whisk (or using a planetary mixer) at least each hour in the freezer until the ice cream reaches the ideal consistency.

Soft Caramel Sauce

175 g / 6 ¼ oz / ¾ cup cane sugar

150 ml / 5 ¼ fl. oz / ⅔ cup fresh cream

30 g butter

pinch of salt

3 tbsp maple syrup

In a thick-bottomed pan, dissolve the sugar with the butter, salt and maple syrup.

Once it has taken on a slightly amber tone, pour in the cream, taking care not to scald yourself as it will spit.

Leave to simmer for a couple of minutes, without stirring but shaking the pan gently.

Caramel and Walnut Ice Cream

Preparation time + freezing for ideal consumption: 5-6 hours

Ingredients for 4-6

220 ml / 7 ¾ fl. oz / 1 cup whole milk

80 ml / 2 ¾ fl. oz / ⅓ cup fresh cream

3 fresh egg yolks

120 g / 4 ¼ oz / ½ cup light cane sugar

seeds of 1 vanilla pod

1 tsp butter

100 g / 3 ½ oz / ⅔ cup walnuts

Warm the butter in a non-stick pan, pour in the walnuts roughly broken up, toss them for a moment and sprinkle with the three spoons of sugar. They must be slightly toasted and caramelised. It will only take a couple of minutes. Once they are ready, turn off the heat and leave to cool.

Place the egg yolks and sugar in the planetary mixer and beat with the whisk until you have obtained a very light and fluffy mixture.

In the meantime, heat the cream and milk with the vanilla seeds and remove from the heat before the mixture starts to boil. Stir to cool slightly, then add to the eggs and sugar, in a slow steady trickle, stirring constantly.

Transfer to the ice cream/sorbet maker and follow the instructions. During the final beating of the ice cream, add the walnuts.

Serve this ice cream with runny caramel and more nuts, in tall glasses.

You can use this basic idea with other nuts. It is perfect with pecans.

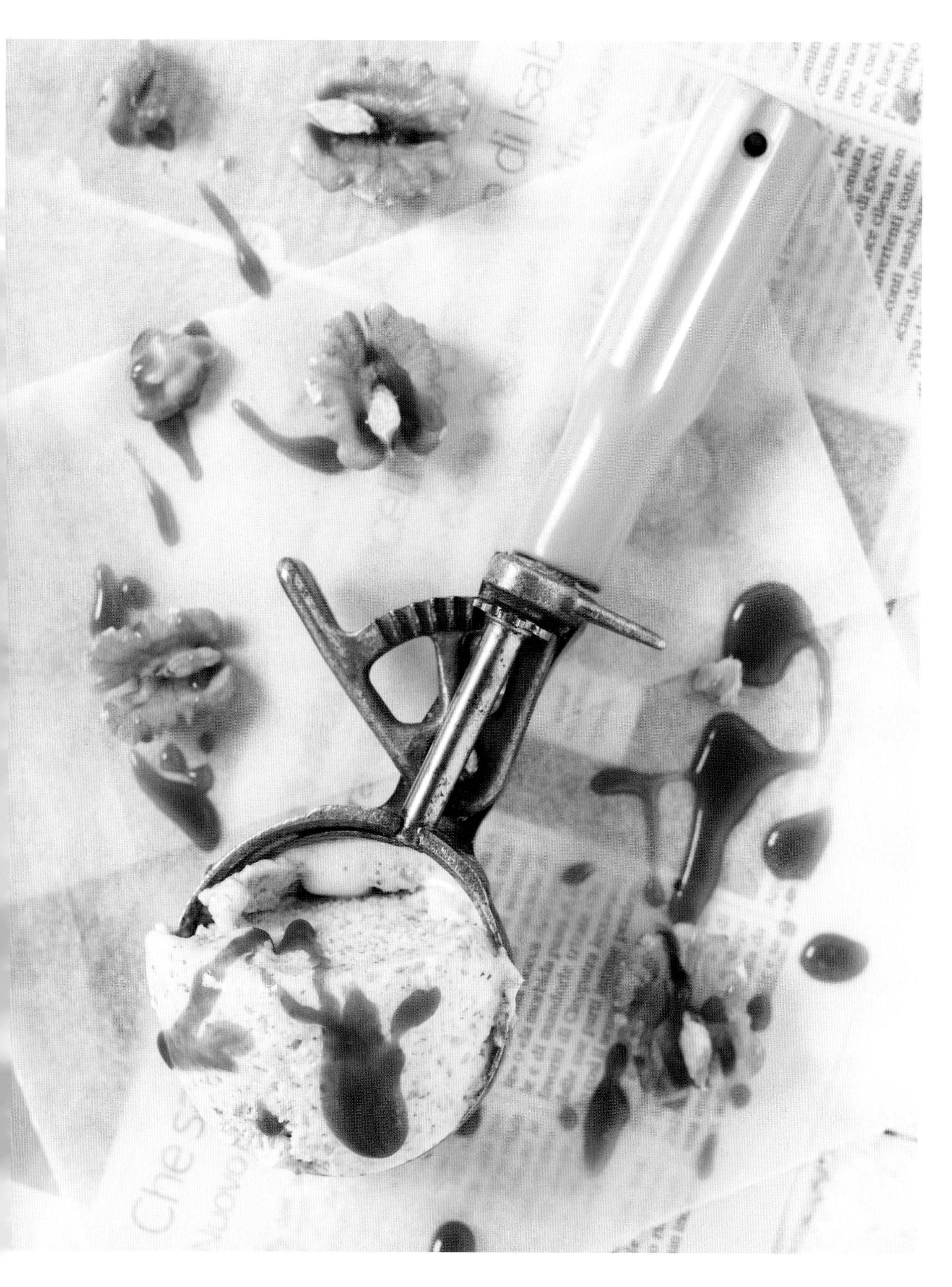

Hazelnut and Chocolate Ripple Ice Cream

Preparation time + freezing for ideal consumption: 12 hours

Ingredients for 4-6

FOR THE ICE CREAM

200 ml / 7 fl. oz / ¾ cup cream

200 ml / 7 fl. oz / ¾ cup whole milk

6 egg yolks

135 g / 4 ¾ oz / ½ cup sugar

250 g / 8 ¾ oz / 2 cups round Piedmont hazelnuts (cob nuts)

FOR THE RIPPLE

130 ml / 4 ½ fl. oz / ½ cup water

105 g / 3 ⅔ oz / ½ cup sugar

25 g cocoa

35 g hazelnut paste

5 g starch

FOR THE ICE CREAM

Roughly chop 100 g / 3 ½ oz of hazelnuts and leave to infuse in the cream overnight.

The next day, place the egg yolks and sugar in the planetary mixer bowl. Beat them with the whisk, at high speed, until you have a creamy, light and fluffy mixture.

Add the filtered cream, pouring it into the egg in a slow steady trickle with the whisk running, and the chilled milk.

Once it has blended well, pour the mixture into a saucepan and stirring constantly with a wooden spoon, simmer over a low heat.

When the custard coats the back of a spoon, remove from the heat immediately and mix until cool.

While you stir, add the hazelnuts that you previously infused in the cream, plus a further 100 g / 3 ½, all roughly chopped.

Finally, place the mixture in the ice cream/sorbet maker and follow the instructions. Towards the end of the beating, add the remaining hazelnuts, whole. Alternatively, if you are doing it manually, beat with an electric whisk (or using a planetary mixer) until the ice cream reaches the ideal consistency.

FOR THE RIPPLE

1 Place the water, sugar, cocoa and bring to the boil, whisking constantly.

2 Remove from the heat, leave to cool for a couple of minutes, and lastly add the hazelnut paste blending carefully.

3 Use this cream to create the ripple in the ice cream.

HOME MADE

CAKES, BISCUITS AND PETIT FOURS

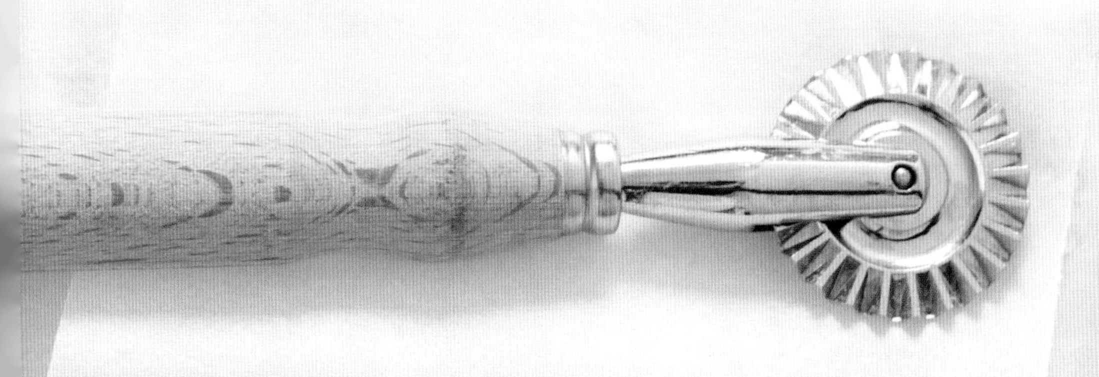

Spiced Biscuit Petit Fours

To prepare these biscuits, the ideal ice cream flavours are fiordilatte, chocolate, pistachio, vanilla custard and coffee, either in their traditional versions or made with plant milks.

Preparation time + freezing for ideal consumption: 5-6 hours

Ingredients for 6-8

FOR THE BISCUITS

50 g / 1 ¾ oz / ⅓ cup rice flour

100 g / 3 ½ oz / ⅔ cup almond flour

100 g / 3 ½ oz / ⅔ cup buckwheat flour

30 g ground hazelnuts (cob nuts)

100 g / 3 ½ oz / ½ cup raw cane sugar

1 tbsp rice syrup or agave syrup

100 ml / 3 ½ fl. oz / 1 cup vanilla flavoured rice milk

80 ml / 2 ¾ fl. oz / ⅓ cup rice oil (or light extra virgin olive oil)

pinch of bicarbonate

1 tsp five-spice powder (or spices for pain d'épices)

ice cream of your choice

Place all the ingredients in the planetary mixer bowl, use the flat beater and beat until you have a smooth mixture. It will be a bit sticky, so sprinkle it with a further dusting of flour (any of those that you are using), bring it together into a ball and place it in the fridge for at least an hour.

After an hour, preheat the oven to 180-200°C / 350-400F / Gas Mark 4 and line a tin with greaseproof paper.

Roll out the dough with a floured rolling pin, cut out some disks or squares with a pastry cutter – if you like decorate them with a stamp – and place them side by side on the tray.

Place them in the oven and check them: as soon as they start to turn golden, take them out. They will seem soft but will harden as they cool.

When they are ready, place a scoop of ice cream in the centre of one biscuit, place a second biscuit on top and press gently. If necessary remove any ice cream that comes out of the sides with a small spatula or knife. Repeat this process until you use up all the biscuits.

Place them in the freezer for about an hour so that they become compact.

Zuccotto

Preparation time + freezing for ideal consumption: 5-6 hours

Ingredients for 4-6

1 sponge with a diameter of at least 20 cm

500 g / 17 $^{2}/_{3}$ oz / 2 cups custard ice cream or lemon ice cream (see basic ice cream recipes in Preparation chapter)

500 g / 17 $^{2}/_{3}$ oz / 2 cups dark chocolate ice cream or fleur de sel and pink pepper ice cream (see basic ice cream recipes in Preparation chapter)

240 ml / 8 ½ fl. oz / 1 cup orange liqueur

VARIATIONS

- Use a chocolate sponge as a base.
- Stuff with fruit ice creams.
- Make a cream with mascarpone and cream and use it as a filling instead of ice cream.
- Stuff with stracciatella ice cream only.
- Use several different ice creams to give different colours and flavours, such as fiordilatte, custard, walnut and chocolate to give a range of tones that have a very appearance, with complementary flavours.

For this dessert, you will need a zucotto mould or dome-shaped bowl.

Cut the sponge into three parts horizontally, then cut it again into 3 cm (1 in) wide strips. Ensure that you have cut a round of the same size as the opening of the mould: you will need it to close the zuccotto. To make it easier to assemble, you can cut the sponge into triangles, just as if it were a cake.

Cover the inside of the mould with layer of cling film: this will help you to get the zuccotto out without any difficulties.

Start to layer the mould with pieces of sponge, taking care not to leave any empty spaces. Follow the lines of the mould. Make the sponge stick in place and gradually soak it with the liqueur using a pastry brush.

When the mould is completely covered on the inside, place it in the freezer for half an hour.

After that time, start to fill the mould about half full with one of the two flavours of ice cream. If you like, you can finish off this half with a few strips of sponge soaked in liqueur.

Place it in the freezer for about an hour.

Now fill the other half of the mould, almost to the brim, with the second flavour of ice cream. Close it, like a lid, with the round of sponge that you set aside.

Leave the zuccotto in the freezer overnight.

The next day, take it out 15 minutes before serving and dust with unsweetened cocoa powder.

You can make the sponge yourself or buy it ready-made.

Panettone stuffed with Ice Cream

Preparation time + freezing for ideal consumption: 5-6 hours

Ingredients for 6-8

1 x 500 g / 17 ⅔ oz classic panettone or 6 x 100g / 3 ½ oz single-serving panettones

470 ml / 16 ½ fl. oz / 2 cups milk

150 g / 5 ⅓ oz / ⅔ cup fresh cream

200 ml / 7 fl. oz / ¾ cup Marsala wine

180 g / 6 ⅓ oz / ¾ cup caster sugar

8 egg yolks

In a glass container, placed over a saucepan to cook in bain-marie, beat the egg yolks and half of the caster sugar, using an electric whisk to get as much air into the mixture as possible. The container should be just touching the water, which must be simmering. The egg yolks should be warmed but not cooked.

When they start to thicken, add the Marsala wine in a slow steady trickle, beating constantly. When the zabaione coats the back of a spoon and is light and fluffy, it is ready. Leave to cool.

In the meantime, lightly whip the cream.

Add the milk to the zabaione in a slow steady trickle, continuing to beat with the whisk, then fold the cream in gently.

Pour the mixture into an ice cream/sorbet maker. Turn it on and follow the instructions. You can beat by hand, using a whisk, every hour for at least four hours. This is a particularly soft and creamy ice cream. If you want to try a different flavour, you can use the same quantity of good aromatic beer or raisin wine instead of the classic Marsala.

Cut the two ends off the panettone. Then, with great care and a sharp knife, try to create a perfect cylinder, cutting out the inside of the panettone and leaving an outer ring at least 2 cm (1 in) thick.

Rest the ring (in other words the hollowed out panettone) on the bottom part and arrange a layer of at least 2 cm (1 in) of ice cream on top. Then cut a slice of the same thickness from the cylinder of panettone and cover with the ice cream, pressing lightly. Continue in this way, finishing with an ice cream layer, until you have finished all the ingredients.

Finally, replace the "dome" of the panettone.

Place the whole thing in the freezer for a couple of hours. When you cut the panettone, you will be guaranteed to surprise your guests! If you heat the oven to the maximum temperature and move the panettone directly from the freezer to the oven, the ice cream will not have time to melt but the external part of the panettone will get very hot, giving you a delightful contrast.

For an original - and very showy - way to present it, stuff the panettone with strawberry ice cream, place mixed berries between the layers and glaze the outside with a layer of real ice, decorated with red fruits.

Lotus

Speculoos Sandwiches

Preparation time + freezing for ideal consumption: 5-6 hours

Ingredients for 4-6

100 g / 3 ½ oz / ½ cup cream

300 g / 10 ½ oz / 1 ¼ cups milk

6 egg yolks

105 g / 3 ⅔ oz / ½ cup caster (superfine) sugar

50 g / 1 ¾ oz / ¼ cup honey

110 g / 4 oz speculoos biscuits + one small pack for the final composition

In the bowl of the planetary mixer place the egg yolks and sugar. Beat them with the whisk at high speed until you have a thick, creamy mixture.

Add the honey, milk and cream to the egg in a slow steady trickle with the whisk running.

Once all the ingredients have blended well, pour the mixture into a saucepan and, stirring constantly with a wooden spoon, simmer over a very low heat.

As soon as the custard coats the back of the spoon, take it off the heat and stir until it is cool.

In the meantime, whizz the biscuits in the blender until they are crumbs and add them to the egg custard, fold in gently and pour into the ice cream/sorbet maker. Alternatively, if you are doing it manually, beat with an electric whisk (or using a planetary mixer) for each hour in the freezer until the ice cream reaches the ideal consistency.

Use the ice cream to join the whole biscuits two by two in "sandwiches".

Cool in the freezer for a couple of hours before serving.

Frozen Passion Fruit Cake

Preparation time + freezing for ideal consumption: 12 hours

Ingredients for 4-6

300 ml / 10 ½ fl. oz / 1 ¼ cups cream

200 g / 7 oz / ¾ cup sugar

250 ml / 8 ¾ fl. oz / 1 cup passion fruit juice

8 egg yolks

1 vanilla pod

juice of 1 lemon

2-3 passion fruits for decoration

To obtain the passion fruit juice, cut the fruit, take out the flesh and place it in a blender, add a tiny drop of water and blend, then filter. The seeds will separate from the flesh and juice.

Place the passion fruit juice, vanilla seeds, sugar, lemon juice in a small pan and over a high heat, let it reduce slightly.

In the bowl of the planetary mixer beat the egg yolks with the whisk until frothy.

Pour in the hot, but not boiling syrup in a slow steady trickle.

Add half of the cream and leaving the whisk running at the highest speed, allow the mixture to increased in volume a little.

Lastly, beat the other half of the cream separately and fold it in gently trying to avoid deflating it, stirring in an upward motion, as you normally would with egg whites.

Pour the mixture into a round cake tin with a 20 cm (8 in) diameter, or into a rectangular one, covered in cling film. Leave in the freezer overnight.

Take the cake out 15 minutes before serving and cut it into slice, decorating with passion fruit flesh or a light raspberry sauce made by blending fresh raspberries with a teaspoon of icing sugar and filtering to get rid of the seeds. Alternatively, prepare single portions, using disposable silicon containers.

Strawberry Bonbons

The filling may be replaced with classics like cream ice cream, special ones such as fruit ice cream or original ones like mint ice cream.

Preparation time + freezing for ideal consumption: 5-6 hours

Ingredients for 4-6

200 g / 7 oz / 1 ⅔ cups dark chocolate

500 g / 17 ⅔ oz / 2 cups strawberry ice cream (or another flavour according to taste)

Melt the chocolate over a bain-marie.

With the help of a pastry brush, coat soft silicon moulds in runny chocolate.

Place in the freezer for 5 minutes, then paint on a "second coat".

After 15 minutes in the freezer, fill the chocolate shells with strawberry ice cream, taking care not to fill up to the top edge, which you will need to seal later.

Leave in the freezer for a couple of hours and with the remaining chocolate, which you will need to melt again, create the "lids" of the bonbons.

You can serve these sweets a couple of hours after making them or prepare them a few days in advance for an special event.

Chestnut Meringues

Preparation time + freezing for ideal consumption: 5-6 hours

Ingredients for 6-8

500 g / 17 ⅔ oz / 2 cups chestnut ice cream (see basic ice cream recipes in Preparation chapter)

FOR THE MERINGUES

2 egg whites

icing sugar, an equal quantity to the weight of the egg whites

2 tsp lemon juice

VARIATIONS

- If you really want to spoil yourself, you can dip the tips of the meringues in a drop of melted dark chocolate and serve with a dollop of whipped cream.
- Alternatively, you can create little fine disks of meringue and make a sort of millefeuille, or form meringue nests to fill with ice cream and then drizzle the surface with melted chocolate.
- You can prepare glasses and crumble the meringue onto scoops of ice cream, not forgetting to add a dollop of fresh whipped cream to make it even more lavish.

Preheat the oven to 50–80°C / 120–175F.

Keep the egg whites at room temperature for around half an hour, then start to beat them, adding the lemon juice a little at a time.

When the whites are very light and fluffy but not yet in stiff peaks, start to add the sugar one spoonful at a time, continuing to beat them all the time (with the planetary mixer or electric whisk). The meringue will be ready to go in the oven when it is almost solid. The classic test are the "stiff peaks" created by the whisk when you lift it. Another test is to turn the bowl upside down and the mixture should not fall out.

Transfer the egg whites to a pastry bag an form many little meringues, with a good space between them, on a baking tray covered in greaseproof paper.

Bake in the oven for about 2–3 hours. If necessary, lower the temperature and extend the cooking time. They should be dry and crispy. One trick is to leave an oven glove in the oven door, so that it does not close completely; this avoids excess moisture.

When the meringues are done, cooled and dry, assemble them in pairs using a teaspoon of chestnut ice cream as "glue". Serve immediately.

Ice Cream Cookies

Preparation time + freezing for ideal consumption: 5-6 hours

Ingredients for 4-6

12 chocolate cookies (or white chocolate cookies)

500 g / 17 ⅔ oz / 2 cups stracciatella ice cream (see basic ice cream recipes in Preparation chapter)

Pour the ice cream onto a baking tray lined with greaseproof paper and smooth out flat with a spatula. You need to reach a thickness of 3-4 cm.

Place it in the freezer for about an hour and then, with a circular pastry cutter of the same size as the cookies, cut out circles and place them between the two cookies. Alternatively, place a scoop of ice cream between the cookies and squash them slightly between your hands, cutting off any excess with a knife. They will not be perfect, but they will be delicious anyway..

You can also use classic, light or vegan biscuits and fill them with chocolate or fruit ice cream.

Homemade Cookies

If you want to make the cookies at home, instead of buying them ready-made, the recipe is easy.

120 g / 4 ¼ oz / ¾ cup flour

100 g / 3 ½ oz / ½ cup sugar

100 g / 3 ½ oz / ½ cup butter

80 g / 2 ¾ oz / ¾ cup unsweetened cocoa (strong)

pinch of salt

pinch of bicarbonate

1 egg

50 g / 1 ¾ oz / ⅓ cup chocolate chips or chopped hazelnuts (cob nuts)

Place the flour, sugar, cocoa, salt, bicarbonate and chilled butter in a bowl. Beat by hand until you have a mixture that resembles breadcrumbs.

Add the egg and mix until you have a smooth and even mixture. Lastly, add the chocolate chips.

Squash the mixture slightly with your hands, wrap in cling film and place in the fridge for about an hour.

Preheat the oven to 180°C.

Dust the work surface with cocoa powder. Roll out the biscuit dough to a thickness of 3-4 mm.

Cut with a pastry cutter in the shape that you prefer and place them on a baking tray lined with greaseproof paper. If you like, prick them with a tooth pick.

Bake them in the oven for about ten minutes, then leave them to cool completely on a wire rack before filling them with the ice cream.

Cheesecake

Preparation time + freezing for ideal consumption: 12 hours

Ingredients for 6-8

FOR THE BISCUIT BASE

150 g / 5 ⅓ oz / 1 ½ cups farro and cocoa biscuits

100 g / 3 ½ oz / 1 cup digestive biscuits

70 g / 2 ½ oz / ⅓ cup melted demi-sel butter

1 tbsp acacia honey

½ tsp five-spice powder

FOR THE CREAM

400 g / 14 oz / 1 ⅔ cups mascarpone

100 g / 3 ½ oz / ½ cup Greek yogurt

150 g / 5 ⅓ oz / ⅔ cup sugar

grated zest of 1 unwaxed lemon

1 tsp vanilla extract

milk (optional)

In the mixer bowl, blend the biscuits to a fine powder, add the honey, spices and melted butter and beat the mixture for a few minutes.

Place a few handfuls of the mixture into a 20 cm (8 in) diameter spring form tin and create the base, pressing down well with your hands.

Place the tin in the fridge for at least 30 minutes.

Beat together the mascarpone, yogurt, sugar, lemon zest and vanilla extract.

Pour the cream mixture onto the biscuit base and place directly in the freezer for a few hours.

Take the cheesecake out of the freezer 15 minutes before serving it and decorating as you like.

DECORATION

- With chocolate: 200 g / 7 oz 65 per cent dark chocolate, 200 ml / 7 fl. oz cream / 2 tbsp maple syrup. Dissolve the chocolate in the cream – ideally over a bain-marie – stir to cool slightly and add the syrup (to make the ganache shiny). Pour this mixture over the cheesecake.
- Instead of a single large cheesecake, make mini portions (using pastry cutters) to decorate with fresh fruit, frosted mixed berries, or chocolate.
- Add a few spoons of passion fruit to the cream and then decorate the surface with a mango and passion fruit glaze: 150 ml / 5 ¼ fl. oz filtered passion fruit juice, 100 g / 3 ½ oz blended mango, 80 g / 2 ¾ oz caster sugar, 50 ml / 1 ¾ fl. oz water. Place all of the ingredients in a saucepan and over a very low heat, leave to reduce until you have a fragrant sauce. Remove from the heat, beat with a whisk to cool an use it to garnish over the cheesecake when you cut it. Or alternatively, when the cheesecake is thoroughly chilled, cover it with the sauce at room temperature and place it back in the freezer.

il Gelato

Index